Date Due

MY GREATEST DAY
IN
FOOTBALL

MY
GREATEST
DAY
IN
FOOTBALL

ALEXANDER · ANDERSON · BATTLES · BAUGH · BELL · BIBLE · BLAIK
BLANCHARD · BROWN · BUTTS · CARIDEO · DAVIS · DOBBS · DUDLEY
EDWARDS · FEATHERS · GIPP · HALAS · HEIN · HERBER · HINKLE · HUTSON
LEAHY · LITTLE · LUCKMAN · OSMANSKI · OWEN · POND · ROCKNE · STAGG
STRONG · STUHLDREHER · THOMAS · WARNER · WATERFIELD · WIEMAN
ZUPPKE

by
MURRAY GOODMAN
and
LEONARD LEWIN
FOREWORD BY LOU LITTLE

A · S · BARNES and COMPANY
New York

Manufactured in the United States of America.

To Bobby Goodman and Johnny Lewin, Mr. Inside and Mr. Outside
of 1968—give or take a few years.

FOREWORD

Football through the years has been our greatest game of body contact.

It is also a game of precision, of self-discipline, of team-play to the ultimate degree. It contains, in my opinion, the elements that make it the finest game ever devised for the American youth to whom competition comes as naturally as the breath of life.

There is another feature of football, especially intercollegiate football, which makes it a valuable part of the American scene. That is the tradition which down through the years has become entwined with the life of our youth and which makes the thud of shoe against pigskin and the piping of the referee's whistle as much a part of the autumn as the change in the foliage on college campuses.

The authors here present what I consider a most interesting addition to the recording of that tradition and the history of football. They take the sport's outstanding contests and, in the words of the men who participated in them either as coach or player, recreate those games in a volume which should find its way into the library of every football enthusiast.

To all of this they add the spice of controversy which always has been and, I hope, always will be a part of football.

My own particular "memorable day," the Rose Bowl classic of January 1, 1934 at Pasadena, California, is a case in point. To this day there are some who can't understand how the courageous Columbia team, a decided underdog, went on to defeat powerful

and highly regarded Stanford. But that's the way football is played.
The imponderables, the emotional qualities which enable a man, or
a group of men, to achieve an objective which had been thought
beyond their powers, are a great part of the game but a part sometimes not easily understood by those who have not played the game.
These are the reasons for what the public light terms "upsets."

It is interesting to see what such football notables as Alonzo
Stagg, Pop Warner, Bob Zuppke and Frank Thomas, representing
a span of more than half a century in the game's history, consider
their outstanding days. You might think it difficult to single out
any one day in a long career but a football coach can do it. Each of
us has had one. That goes also for the players—Frank Carideo, Sid
Luckman, Don Hutson and the others—stars who have seen action
and thrills through season after season against the best in the game.
Some of their selections of their "greatest day" may surprise you.

Together, the coaches and the players have enabled the authors
to put together a book including the thrills of many of those who
have made a permanent contribution to football.

I am sure you'll like it.

LOU LITTLE

ACKNOWLEDGMENTS

To the many college sports publicity directors, the unsung heroes of many a football team. Their assistance has been invaluable.

To the Sports Writers, always cooperative, who helped fill in the inevitable gaps.

To the coaches and players—college and professional—without whom this book could never have been written.

To Don Schiffer, of the deft and discerning editing hand, and other members of the A. S. Barnes & Co. editorial staff, and production department who were both patient and obliging.

CONTENTS

WILLIAM A. (BILL) ALEXANDER
(*Georgia Tech, '11*)
GEORGIA TECH, 1912-1944.

When Bill Alexander hung up his coaching mantle in 1944, after 33 years of coaching at Georgia Tech, the Georgia House of Representatives adopted a resolution commending him for his "accomplishments in behalf of the young men of this State."

Alexander, who now restricts his duties to Director of Athletics, a job he has had since 1921 in addition to coaching football, is one of the South's greatest contributions to intercollegiate football.

Rarely more than a "scrub" as an undergrad, Alexander absorbed a wealth of knowledge under the great John W. Heisman and taught with huge success. He not only coached the Yellow Jackets to six Southern Conference championships, but also produced four Bowl teams, of which three triumphed.

His 1928 team won 10 games in an undefeated, untied season and then whipped California, 8 to 7, in a Rose Bowl game made famous by Roy "Wrong Way" Riegels. The 1939 eleven toppled Missouri in the Orange Bowl, 21 to 7, and the 1943 machine won a Sugar Bowl thriller from Tulsa, 20 to 18. His only Bowl defeat came in January, 1943, when Texas took a 14-7 Cotton Bowl decision.

The 1942 team might have been the greatest in Tech history but after winning nine straight, it took a humiliating, 34-0, trouncing from Georgia. Even then, the Yellow Jackets were ranked fifth nationally. Alexander was voted Coach of the Year in 1942 to climax a splendid career.

A fine wit, Alexander is a "must" speaker wherever football coaches gather.

BILL ALEXANDER
Georgia Tech 20, Tulsa 18.
SUGAR BOWL, NEW ORLEANS, LA., JANUARY 1, 1944.

This is the story of a war-woven football team—the tale of an aggregation of carefree sailors who laid no claims to greatness yet wrote one of the greatest chapters into the history of Georgia Tech football.

The record shows that Georgia Tech won seven and lost three during the 1943 season but this is one case where you can safely say "let's not look at the record." For this Golden Tornado eleven, a collection of Navy Nomads, not only gave me my greatest day in football but produced one of the mightiest victories in our gridiron annals when they came from behind in the last eight minutes to defeat the Hurricanes of Tulsa, 20 to 18, in the Sugar Bowl of January 1, 1944.

Winning that Sugar Bowl classic actually was the climax of one of the strangest seasons I've ever had in my many years of coaching. War has a way of doing things, even to football teams, and when the season began I didn't know what to look forward to—or whether I'd have a football squad to field. Most of my players were part of the Navy V-12 program, and they were coming and leaving so fast, that I doubted the wisdom of teaching them signals. They came from all over, some with football experience but all unfamiliar with me or my system. Only two men, Prokop and Beall, were my heritage from the 1942 eleven.

*Football's rules makers of 1944: Bill Alexander, Georgia Tech.;
Harry Stuhldreher, Wisconsin; Lou Little, Columbia; Fritz Crisler,
Michigan; Bernie Moore, Louisiana State.*

The lineup of the team that took the field in November is significant enough:

L.E.	Tinsley, Alabama freshman in 1942.
L.T.	Chambers, Alabama varsity in 1942.
L.G.	Steber (Captain) Vanderbilt varsity in 1942.
C.	Cummings, Vanderbilt varsity in 1942.
R.G.	Beall, Georgia Tech varsity in 1942.
R.T.	Phillips, Texas A & M freshman in 1942.
R.E.	Kilzer, Vanderbilt varsity in 1942.
Q.B.	Faulkner, Georgia Tech B squad in 1942.
L.H.	Prokop, Georgia Tech varsity in 1942.
R.H.	Logan, Georgia Tech freshman in 1942.
F.B.	Scharfschwerdt, Georgia Tech freshman in 1942.

My good friend Gus Welch, quarterback of the Carlisle Indians in the days of Jim Thorpe, tells a story that aptly describes my 1943 eleven.

"I was the reason for Carlisle's success," Welch declares modestly. "It was simple. Pop Warner used to tell me to give the ball to Thorpe and then block for him. My instructions were to hit the end, and, if I missed him, to go on to the next man. So I'd miss the end, head for the backer-up, miss him and then go for the safety. The next thing I knew, I'd be standing in the end-zone alongside Thorpe and we'd have a touchdown."

If ever there was a hit-or-miss team, it was my Ramblin' Wrecks of 1943.

We started the season convincingly enough with a victory over North Carolina, then took a terrific 55-13 drubbing from Notre Dame. Georgia Pre-Flight and Fort Benning fell before our experimental forces as things looked brighter but along came Navy to wallop us, 28 to 14, and we dropped a close one to Duke, 14 to 7.

Following the Duke game, we lost a few of our good players to the active Navy and it seemed that Georgia Tech was headed for its worst season. The fates are funny, however. Suddenly, we became an overnight sensation. We slaughtered Louisiana State, 42 to 7, trounced Tulane, 33 to 0, romped over Clemson, 41 to 6, and finished the season by murdering Georgia 48 to 0—the same Georgia that had ruined a perfect record for us the year before in the closing game of the season. We were hitting on all V-12's.

That last victory brought us the invitation to the Sugar Bowl against Coach Henry Frnka's famous "4-F" team which had gone through seven games with six victories and one tie. Tulsa's boys were all handicapped physically to the point of Army and Navy disability but there was nothing wrong with their football ability. They had a one-armed guard—Jones—who was good enough to gain All-America mention. He was fast and block-tackled our Tars off their feet with as much power as any lineman on the field.

Instead of going direct to New Orleans to prepare for the game, I sent the boys home for Christmas. This might be their last Christmas at home. They all met me in New Orleans on schedule—all except Bill Chambers. He was washed off a plane by priority and arrived, broke and hungry, by train the day before the game.

My generosity in giving them a vacation seemed to backfire in the first half. Led by the 165-pound bundle of dynamite, Clyde LeForce, Tulsa swept through the Yellow Jackets for a touchdown in the first five minutes as LeForce passed to Shedlosky. In the second period, pint-sized Jimmy Ford raced 76 yards—the longest touchdown run in Sugar Bowl history—and we trailed 12 to 0. We came back momentarily when Broyles cracked over from a foot out to top a 61-yard drive but Tulsa scored again before the half was over. Ford kicked a beautiful 68-yarder to our six and Broyles fumbled. Tulsa recovered and LeForce skirted end to make it Tulsa, 18, Georgia Tech, 7. The Hurricanes had turned the Golden Tornado into a mild zephyr.

There have been many stories of half-time speeches by coaches to inspire teams on the verge of defeat. I made no orations. They were naturally downcast in the dressing room. They were in no mood for a lecture. I waited until the last moment without saying much. And then, I said simply:

"If you want your beer, fellows, you'd better go out and win this game."

I doubt if the beer itself was the spark that ignited the fuse. The curtain of tension was lifted, however. The team that played the second half of that ball game was once again the machine that roared through its last four games of the season.

Eddie Prokop never gained All-America honors at Georgia Tech but he was among the best in that dramatic second half. We switched from a passing game, which had proved futile in the opening quarters, and battered our way on the ground. Prokop did most of the carrying and with the amazing John Steber blocking, moved into Tulsa territory. The Tulsa defense packed tightly to halt our rushing game but Prokop crossed them by tossing to Tinsley on their 30 and the big end took it the rest of the way. Prokop's kick failed and it was 18 to 13.

On defense, too, Steber was a superb player, and backed by Chambers, Phillips and Cummings, a 60-minute center, thwarted every Tulsa offensive in the fourth quarter. But Tulsa was just as stubborn. It was a bruising battle of lines that refused to budge—until we took possession on our own 21 with eight minutes left.

Then Prokop went to town. That march of 79 yards will always remain in my mind. Prokop smashed the line, rounded the ends, picking up yard after yard, and always with big Steber paving the way. There was no stopping either of them. Ten plays put the ball on the one-foot line and from there, Scharfschwerdt battered across for the winning touchdown. Prokop added the point to make it complete. He gained 199 yards rushing that afternoon.

The boys had their beer that night and I had my greatest thrill.

The lineup:

GEORGIA TECH (20)	pos.	TULSA (18)
Tinsley	le	Herriman
Chambers	lt	Burgeis
Steber	lg	E. Jones
Cummings	c	Prewitt
Hoover	rg	Buda
Phillips	rt	Stanley
Kilzer	re	Goodnight
Faulkner	qb	Taylor
Prokop	lh	LeForce
Logan	rh	Shedlosky
Broyles	fb	Wilson

Georgia Tech .... 0—7—6—7——20
Tulsa .... 6—12—0—0——18

Touchdowns: *Georgia Tech*—Broyles, Tinsley, Scharfschwerdt (sub for Faulkner). *Tulsa*—Shedlosky, LeForce, Ford (sub for Taylor).

Points after touchdowns: *Georgia Tech*—Prokop, 2.

Substitutions: *Tulsa*—Lunn, Stegman, White, Butterworth, Leagreca, Gray, D. Jones, Minauk, Wade, B. Smith, A. Smith, Kowalski, Ford, Walker. *Georgia Tech*—Dorough, Bourne, Mills, Beall, Furchgott, Gaston, Scharfschwerdt, Wakefield.

DR. EDWARD N. (EDDIE) ANDERSON
(*Notre Dame, '22*)
COLUMBIA COLLEGE, DUBUQUE, IOWA, 1922-1924.
DE PAUL, CHICAGO, 1925-1931.
HOLY CROSS, 1933-1938.
IOWA, 1939-1942, 1946-　.

Eddie Anderson, a full-fledged Doctor of Medicine with football in his blood, got his winning habits under the immortal Knute Rockne at Notre Dame. He was an end, and a good one, on the teams of 1918, 1919, 1920 and 1921, with unbeaten seasons in 1919 and 1920—and a winning streak which ended at 20 at the hands of Iowa in 1921. In 1939, ironically enough, his first year as coach of the Iowa Hawkeyes, he ended another Irish string of triumphs.

Steeped in the tradition of football not only under so great a teacher as Rockne but with such teammates as George "The Gipper" Gipp, Hunk Anderson, Harry Mehre, Buck Shaw, Frank Thomas, Slip Madigan, among others, Anderson gained national repute with his record at Holy Cross. In six years as Crusader leader, his teams won 47, lost seven, and tied four, with an undefeated season in 1935, the first in Holy Cross football history, and only a tie with Manhattan came along to mar the record.

There was no doubt about Anderson's coaching ability or his inspirational leadership after the 1939 season. His selection as "Coach of the Year" was well earned. He took an Iowa team that had won one game, lost six and tied one in 1938, and not only gained ninth place in the National ranking but accounted for two of the biggest upsets of the year—victories over mighty Notre Dame and Minnesota.

Anderson had a hand in developing two outstanding All-America players—Bill Osmanski at Holy Cross, and Nile Kinnick, a boy who traded a gold helmet for a gold star, at Iowa. Anderson, too, saw wartime service, leaving his Iowa post in 1942 and returning in 1946.

EDDIE ANDERSON
Iowa 7, Notre Dame 6.
IOWA CITY, IA., NOVEMBER 11, 1939.

Notre Dame vs. Iowa.

My alma mater against the school I was coaching for the first year.

Final score: Iowa, 7; Notre Dame, 6.

With Iowa leading by one point in the fourth quarter, with the pressure on deep in his own territory, Nile Kinnick, Iowa's great All-America back, dropped into punt formation and booted one of the most beautiful kicks I've ever seen, for 72 yards, virtually assuring victory for Iowa. One of the most brilliant of all football careers ended when Kinnick died serving his country in 1942.

This game was supposed to be a breather for the undefeated Irish. Under Elmer Layden, they had won six straight games, heading for their first undefeated season since Knute Rockne's national champions of 1930. And, strangely enough, it was an Iowa team coached by Howard Jones, which beat Notre Dame, 10 to 7, in 1921, to end a 20-game winning streak. I was captain and end of that Notre Dame eleven.

This must have been a game of destiny. Notre Dame had won four games that year by the margin of an extra point or a field goal. This one the Irish lost because they failed to kick an extra point.

Iowa, winner of only one game in 1938, and doormat of the Western Conference for a long time, was a much underrated team

Eddie Anderson shows why coaches get gray as he watches his Iowa Hawkeyes allow an end to get through.

that afternoon even against so strong an eleven as the Ramblers. Only Michigan had beaten us in five games—the Hawkeyes best record since 1929—and with Kinnick at his best Iowa was always a possibility.

Iowa was a team of "Iron Men" that day. Kinnick was playing his fifth straight game without relief, while seven others went through the entire 60 minutes of holding the Irish.

Forty seconds before the first half ended, the Hawkeyes took advantage of one of the queerest "breaks" I've seen on a football field, and turned it into what proved to be the winning margin. Iowa was in a scoring position for the first and only time of the game. Kinnick faded back to pass. It was a long pass and went into the end zone where Steve Sitko, Irish safety, moved up to intercept it. With only a minute of the half left, Sitko raced the ball back onto the playing field, and then, for no apparent reason—as he saw himself cornered by onrushing Hawkeyes—he tried a lateral.

Bruno Andruska, Iowa center, hit Sitko hard and the ball went flying. Both Dick Evans and Floyd Dean pounced on it, and Iowa had the ball on Notre Dame's four-yard line.

First, Kinnick, then Dean, tried to break the Irish line without a gain. Then Kinnick shifted over to right-halfback from his usual left half post, hit over the Irish right tackle—and there was the touchdown. Kinnick proceeded to dropkick the extra point and it was that margin which gave us the game.

Milt Piepul scored for the Irish on a four-yard cutback through center on the second play of the fourth period and it appeared that the Hawkeyes brilliant line stand would go before a belated avalanche. But Lou Zontini, the big halfback noted for his amazing accuracy and efficiency with the toe, chose this opportune moment for us to make one of his rare misses for the extra point. The kick went to the left of the goal posts and the lead still belonged to Iowa.

The Irish tried but Iowa wasn't giving up what destiny seemed to have forecast for that day. And when Kinnick's tremendous boot of 72 yards broke up the last of the Notre Dame threats, we knew that victory was ours.

How great Kinnick was—and I've seen perhaps the best in Notre Dame's own George "The Gipper" Gipp, my teammate—was evidenced a week later in a game that gave me another heart throb. There were 50,000 people in our stands to watch Minnesota tear us apart, and for the better part of four periods that's exactly what they did. Our "Iron Men" were folding up before a merciless onslaught but never did that indomitable spirit of theirs yield.

The score was 9 to 0 in favor of the Gophers as the fourth period started ticking away but Kinnick and his charges never stopped trying. This same Kinnick, who had been unable to make a solid gain for 45 minutes, suddenly started to move. He pitched and he smashed and then with a horde of Gopher tacklers virtually upon him, passed again to Captain Erwin Prasse for the touchdown. It was Minnesota 9, Iowa 7, after Kinnick's successful dropkick.

With the clock racing, Iowa fought desperately to gain possession of the ball again. It did, with five minutes remaining, and then Kinnick proved he was not only a great player but a fine tactician. We had rehearsed a play in which Bill Green was to be a decoy for Buzz Dean and Prasse on passes. Green was fast and had to be watched closely. Prasse and Dean were alternately the pass receivers. The time was ripe to make use of the decoy and that Kinnick did. He fired one pass to Dean, for a 17-yard gain from his own 21, and then overshot to Prasse. Interference was called against Minnesota and the ball was ours on the 45.

Two rushing plays set up the finale. Green set out again as decoy, with Dean in tow. Dean never got the ball. It went to the blazing Green—a tremendous pass into the end zone that was caught just as Gophers overwhelmed Kinnick and crushed him to the ground. Minnesota was beaten, 13 to 9, in a game that saw strong men weep at the sheer drama of the occasion. They carried the boy with the golden helmet gleaming in the sun off the field on a thousand shoulders.

I've had many great days as a player and many great days as a coach. I once thought my greatest thrill was racing down to recover our own kickoff which helped Notre Dame beat Nebraska, 7 to 0, in 1921, or catching Gipp's bullet passes in 1920, but I doubt if I'll ever experience again the glory of the day that Nile Kinnick gave me in 1939.

They named me Coach of the Year in 1939 but there is no doubt that the glory belonged to Iowa and Kinnick, the best football player of 1939 and one of the greatest and most courageous I have ever seen.

The lineup:

IOWA (7)	pos.	NOTRE DAME (6)
Prasse	le	Biagi
Bergstrom	lt	Brutz
K. Pettit	lg	Defrance
Andruska	c	McIntyre
Snider	rg	Riffle
Enich	rt	Lillis
Evans	re	J. Kelly
Couppee	qb	Sitko
Kinnick	lh	Stevenson
McLain	rh	Crimmins
Murphy	fb	Thesing

Iowa .... 0—7—0—0——7
Notre Dame .... 0—0—0—6——6

Touchdowns: *Iowa*—Kinnick. *Notre Dame*—Piepul (sub for Thesing).

Point after touchdown: *Iowa*—Kinnick (dropkick).

Substitutions: *Iowa*—Tollefson, Hawkins, Dean, Green. *Notre Dame*—Kerr, O'Brien, Arboit, Albert, Brose, P. Kelly, Gubanish, Lasker, Finneran, Juzwik, Hargrave, Saggau, Zontini, Piepul, Bagarus, Kelleher, Sheridan, O'Meara.

Referee—Jim Masker, Northwestern. Umpire—John Schommer, Chicago. Field Judge—Lyle Clarno, Bradley Tech. Head Linesman—E. C. Krieger, Ohio U.

CLIFFORD FRANKLYN (CLIFF) BATTLES
(*West Virginia Wesleyan, '32*)
WASHINGTON REDSKINS, 1932-1937.
COLUMBIA, 1938-1943.
EL TORO MARINES, 1944.
BROOKLYN DODGERS, 1946-1947.

The greatest runner ever produced by a minor college—that honor belongs to Cliff Battles.

The slim, tightly-knit all-around athlete probably covered more distance on the way to touchdown runs than any other college athlete. Against Waynesburg College, in 1930, the Akron, Ohio youth streaked to touchdowns with gallops of 98, 96 and 82 yards. The year before he had scoring dashes of 55 and 45 yards in one game, and 85, 75 and 50 yards in another. These sensational runs made only local headlines but when Battles rolled up 400 yards and seven touchdowns in a 1930 battle with Salem College, and touchdowns on distances of 90, 75 and 70 yards against Georgetown, and sped 70 and 65 yards against New York University, he became a national figure.

Starring in baseball, basketball, tennis, track and swimming as well as football did not prevent Battles from being a Phi Beta Kappa student. He carried his athletic prowess into the pro field. Two of his National Football League records still remain—most yards gained in a game, 215 in 16 attempts against the Giants in 1933, and most ball-carrying attempts in a season, 216 for 874 yards in 1937.

He joined the Redskins when Boston was their home in 1932 and moved with them to Washington in 1937. There, he teamed with Sammy Baugh to bring a championship to the Redskins and all-league honors for both him and Baugh. Battles also made the all-league team in 1933 and 1936.

Cliff became a Marine in 1943. He returned to civilian status and succeeded Mal Stevens as coach of the Brooklyn Dodgers of the All-America Conference on November 1, 1946. An excellent coach, Battles was hampered by lack of material and his departure from Brooklyn was inevitable. The Battles name, however, will undoubtedly continue to be a strong active force in football, college or pro.

CLIFF BATTLES
Washington Redskins 49, New York Giants 14.
NEW YORK, DECEMBER 5, 1937.

The Boston Redskins, a somehow ill-fated team which never had either the support or the cheers of the Boston fans, moved to Washington in 1937, and no college could duplicate the spirit or the feats of the Capitol fandom. We invaded New York on December 5th, our first appearance in the Polo Grounds as the Redskins—and the game meant the Eastern Division championship. If we won, we were in—if we lost, it meant a tie with the Giants and a playoff. We were out to win.

Probably the most fantastic maneuvers in all football history preceded our entry onto the playing field for the game that John Kieran called "The Massacre at Coogan's Bluff." So great was the spirit of Washington fans, they arrived in New York in countless numbers. Some came by automobile over the 225-mile distance, others by bus. They chartered railroad coaches and special trains. The trains bore every evidence of Washington faith. Placards reading "Sammy Baugh Club," others "Cliff Battles Club,"—there were clubs for almost every member of our high-riding squad—and even the New York subways were tagged with "Redskin Special." Red feathers with "Redskins" painted in gold stuck out in thousands of male and female hatbands.

And then there was the astounding brass band which started from Penn Station. Bedecked in costumes of burgundy and gold, with headdresses of white feathers, and led by two drum majors, the bandsmen woke the town with their "Hail to the Redskins." They paraded from Penn Station to Columbus Circle, some 25 blocks, and right with them in his raccoon coat was George Marshall, Redskin owner. Almost the entire contingent of 10,000 loyal fans dragged along behind. They tell me that Marshall cried over the scene.

With this as a setting, we took the field against the stubborn Giants for an all-important game. We had beaten them 13 to 3 in the opening game of the season and looked ahead to another fierce struggle.

Nobody in that crowd of 58,000 expected the rout that followed. It was the second largest crowd in the history of pro football at the time and it saw a great team have one of those exceptional days against an eleven that never gave up regardless of the score. Those Giants were tough and rough.

We jumped to a 14 to 0 lead in the first quarter and increased

Cliff Battles, Sammy Baugh and Wayne Millner after the Washington Redskins' championship 28-21 victory over the Chicago Bears, 1937.

it to 21 by the end of the half. It was in the third period that the Giants made their dramatic stand, with the brilliant Ward Cuff grabbing a ball off my fingertips on a pass from Ed Danowski intended for Will Walls. Cuff raced 62 yards for the first Giant score. Danowski to Tuffy Leemans gave them their other touchdown and the Giant fans in the crowd went crazy. But it just wasn't in the books for the Giants that day.

Baugh was magnificent with his passes and the heave that broke the Giant backs was one to Ed Justice for 43 yards and a touchdown late in the third period. And the remarkable Turk Edwards produced the next one for us when he boomed in to block a Danowski punt. The ball bounded off the massive Edwards chest and skidded into the end zone where Wayne Millner promptly fell on it for a score.

The "breaks" seemed to be against the Giants but it was a mighty Redskin eleven that played that ball game—a team geared to a fever pitch. I do not deny that I was thrilled over the newspaper reports of my own part in the proceedings but my contribution was purely as part of an inspired, well-oiled machine. "No greater back ever appeared in the Polo Grounds than the one-time West Virginia Wesleyan ace," they said, and I'm tremendously proud of their tribute particularly since that year happened to be my last as a player in the professional sport.

I scored our first touchdown on a two-yard plunge in the opening period, but it was a perfect pass from Baugh to me that had put us into payoff territory. The second score followed my 75-yard run on a reverse and I must have been a little slow on that one because Cuff, a great defensive player, pulled me down from behind. I scored a moment later on another stab over the goal-line.

Max Krause scored our third touchdown, but the deciding score of that game belonged to Baugh and Justice on their magnificent pass play. With the game over as far as the score was concerned, I intercepted a pass by Hank Soar midway in the final period, and by dint of great blocking by my teammates, managed to run it all the way to the Giant one-yard line—76 yards—where Les Corzine pushed me out of bounds. Twice I had to reverse my field on this run and it seemed to me that I must have covered about twice the length of the field doing it. On the next play, Riley Smith went over. Just to add to the Giant woes, Smith pulled a "Baugh" and pitched to

Millner for the final touchdown of the game and kicked his seventh straight extra point as the game ended.

This game is important to me because of many factors and I will never forget it. It was my last "great day" as a football player from a purely personal feeling although I got a tremendous kick out of being a member of the team that beat the Chicago Bears for Washington's first world championship the following week. And, of course, it brought back memories of my days at West Virginia Wesleyan—the inflamed spirit of fans and·players alike. I doubt if I'll ever again witness in professional football the fighting, undaunted desire to win as a team for a city as the Washington Redskins of 1937. My association with the Redskins will always remain among my fondest memories, particularly that ball game against the Giants.

The lineup:
WASHINGTON

(49)	pos.	NEW YORK (14)
Millner	le	Poole
Edwards	lt	Widseth
Olsson	lg	Del Isola
G. Smith	c	Hein
Karcher	rg	Tuttle
Barber	rt	Grant
Malone	re	Howell
R. Smith	qb	Leemans
Battles	lh	Danowski
Baugh	rh	Cuff
Pinckert	fb	Corzine
Washington	14—7—7—21——49	
New York	0—0—14—0——14	

Touchdowns: *Washington*—Battles, 2, Millner, 2, Krause, Justice, R. Smith. *New York*—Cuff, Leemans.

Points after touchdown: *Washington*—R. Smith, 7. *New York* —Manton, 2.

Substitutions: *Redskins*—McChesney, B. Smith, Bond, Carroll, Young, Michaels, H. Krause, Butt, Justice, M. Krause, Howell. *Giants*—Walls, Hanken, Haden, Parry, Dennerlein, White, Lunday, Galazin, Kobroskey, Richards, Soar, Manton, Burnett, Shaffer.

Referee—Tom Thorp. Umpire—Tom Hughitt. Linesman—W. T. Halloran. Field Judge—Dr. B. A. O'Hara.

SAM (SLINGIN' SAMMY) BAUGH
(*Texas Christian, '37*)
WASHINGTON REDSKINS, 1937-   .

"*Hey, look at me! I'm Sammy Baugh.*"

Thus the kids of America have elected the Sweetwater, Texas, product to sports immortality alongside heroes like Babe Ruth, Lou Gehrig, Jack Dempsey, Red Grange and company.

"*Slingin' Sammy*" Baugh has established himself in both collegiate and professional fields as one of the greatest—if not the greatest—forward passers of all-time. In 1935 and 1936, when he earned All-America honors in the backfield of Texas Christian University's Horned Frogs, he was already thrilling fans with his superbly and amazingly accurate passing. And when he was passing, they forgot that here, too, was a mighty defensive player as well as a long and dangerous punter.

Baugh joined the Washington Redskins in 1937 and his value to the 'Skins is reflected in their record since then—reaching the championship playoffs in five of his 10 seasons and winning National League crowns in 1937, 1940 and 1943. And in his other years, the Redskins have three times finished second and third an equal number of seasons. All of which gained Baugh All-League honors in 1937, 1940 and 1945.

Responsible for the majority of points scored by Washington in his career with them, Baugh has tallied only 13 points on his own. He ran for touchdowns on two occasions and kicked one extra point. While his passing far overshadows everything he has ever done in football—he has set records that will take years to erase, if ever—he is regarded as the league's best quick-kicker and also owns punts of 85 and 83 yards in distance. A halfback during most of his college days, Baugh has firmly established himself as one of the top quarterbacks in professional history.

Picking an All-Time, All-America, pro or college regardless of position played, Grantland Rice and a group of prominent coaches listed twelve greats who couldn't be left off any team—and among those twelve was Baugh—Mr. Forward Pass.

SAMMY BAUGH
Washington Redskins 28, Chicago Bears 21.
NATIONAL LEAGUE CHAMPIONSHIP, CHICAGO, DECEMBER 12, 1937.

For the one game that gave me my greatest day in football, I'll have to stick with the National League Championship game in wh . the Redskins beat the mighty Chicago Bears, 28 to 21. I've had many thrills and what one might call "great days" but that one turned out to be something special—possibly because the victory gave the Redskins what was then considered the world's pro championship—and that year happened to be my first in the professional ranks.

I'll never forget the setting for that ball game in Wrigley Field. Three days before the game, it snowed, leaving the ground like a skating rink and certainly in no shape for a football game. The field had been covered with a tarpaulin and straw to protect it from the snow but the bitter cold, a wild northwest wind and other tricks of the elements revealed a solid sheet of ice when the covering was removed at game time.

Both teams wore tennis shoes or sneakers to prevent skidding, but we were sliding all over the place right from the start. Our great Cliff Battles, who was so superb against the Giants in the Eastern division clincher the week before, was hobbled by the uncertain footing.

This must have been my day. I couldn't do anything wrong— but this was definitely the roughest game of football I ever played

Mr. Forward Pass—Sammy Baugh.

in. Those Bears, with such great bone-crushing ground gainers as Bronko Nagurski, Jack Manders and Ray Nolting, had a situation made to order for straightaway running and bursts through the middle but we scored first, early in the opening period. Hemmed in in our own end zone, completely surrounded by rough, roaring Bears, I spotted Battles and heaved one 42 yards. The reliable Cliff caught it and seconds later scored on a sweeping reverse from the seven-yard line.

Fingers numb in this zero weather that held even Chicago's rabid fans down to 15,000, we had to rub them continually to keep the circulation going. The Bears, however, seemed unbothered either by the cold or our opening touchdown. They plunged and hammered away at us with unrelenting savageness. In four successive plays they ploughed through us for 71 yards and one touchdown, and shortly afterward, in four more plays, they went 50 yards for another, Manders scoring each time. The first half ended with the Bears leading 14 to 7. I was limping badly from a bruise I'd received in the second period.

They said the Bears were out to get me, but that can't be true. I was a key man and they were doing their utmost to throttle my passes and bottle me up. That they didn't is a fine tribute not to me but to ends like Wayne Millner and Ed Justice, who caught passes almost blindfolded, and to a line led by mighty Turk Edwards, Jim Barber and the rest. That's football.

With my leg in bad shape, they almost wouldn't let me get back in for the third quarter but I hobbled back. We scored the tying touchdown in the first five plays as the elusive Millner caught one of my passes in a 55-yard splurge. Then, the Bears started to march again. We stopped the battering-ram on the three-yard line but Masterson passed to Manske for the score anyway, and it was Bears 21, Redskins 14. That thermometer was still 0 and so seemed our chances.

Riley Smith returned the kickoff to our 23-yard line and, on the next play, I passed 29 yards to Millner. The former Notre Dame star was not dropping any nor was he letting any Bears tag him. He raced 48 more yards for the touchdown that once more tied the knot, this time at 21-all.

As the game progressed, the Bears were swarming over me in ever-rougher hordes. They were also watching Charley Malone, our other end, on the play that won the game for us. Malone cut down the field with Chicagoans all around him. I faded back, on the run, and still on the run, heaved the ball—but not to Malone. Justice was in the right flat and there was absolutely no doubt about where he was headed when he put his arms around that ball. I completed 18 out of 33 passes that day for 335 yards, still a National League play-off record.

We played alert, hard football that day, too. Perhaps I played a little too hard. It would have been entirely an anti-climax for a game like that to end on a peaceful note. In the fourth period, with our main efforts turned to holding down the desperate, clawing Bears, and maintaining our slim lead, Dick Plasman caught a pass from Bernie Masterson and with a clear field ahead, was on his way. I wasn't too far behind and to make sure of getting him, whirled him out of bounds at midfield—right into the middle of the Redskin bench. Plasman must have thought my roughness was intentional. He threw a punch at me and what happened immediately afterward I'll never forget although the details are vague in the excitement that followed.

They tell me that George Marshall, the Redskin owner, screamed:

"They've hit Baugh!"

As Marshall charged onto the field, so did the Bear reserves. Fans, too, jumped over the rail onto the field, and from all parts of the field, people were yelling: "Riot! Riot!"

Policemen swarmed into the fray to untangle the mass of arms and legs. Marshall grabbed me and finding I was still alive and breathing very quickly ushered me to the bench and then rushed back. When the all-clear bell sounded, there were still two men fighting—verbally—George Marshall and George Halas, owner and coach of the Bears. Off the field, they are the best of friends, but here they were screaming threats at each other and it threatened to start another battle. A shot boomed out above the noise, however, and this is one gun that ended a fight. The gun had gone off ending the game, and amid bruised bodies, frost-bitten hands, and flaring tempers, Washington emerged with its first world's professional championship.

It was all the way, a bitter, battering game—my greatest day in football.

The lineup:

WASHINGTON

(28)	pos.	CHICAGO (21)
Millner	le	Manske
Edwards	lt	Stydahar
Olsson	lg	Fortmann
Kawal	c	Bausch
Karcher	rg	Musso
Barber	rt	Bjork
Malone	re	Wilson
R. Smith	qb	Masterson
Baugh	lh	Nolting
Pinckert	rh	Manders
Battles	fb	Nagurski
Redskins	7—0—21—0——28	
Bears	14—0—7—0——21	

Touchdowns: *Washington*—Battles, Millner, 2, Justice. *Chicago* —Manders, 2, Manske.

Points after touchdowns: *Washington*—R. Smith, 4. *Chicago*— Manders, 3.

Substitutions: *Redskins*—Bond, Young, Carroll, Michaels, Kahn, G. Smith, Justice, Irwin, Krause. *Bears*—Plasman, Karr, Mc-Donald, Thompson, Zeller, Conkright, Molesworth, Ronzani, Rentner, Buivid, Francis, Feathers.

Referee—W. T. Halloran, Providence. Umpire—E. W. Cochrane, Chicago. Field Judge—E. F. Hughitt, Buffalo. Linesman —Bobby Cahn, Chicago.

MADISON (MATTY) BELL
(*Centre, '19*)
HASKELL INDIANS, 1919-1921.
CARROLL COLLEGE, 1922.
TEXAS CHRISTIAN, 1923-1928.
TEXAS A & M, 1929-1934.
SOUTHERN METHODIST, 1935-   .

Regardless of what the future holds for him, Matty Bell has been a Southwest football immortal since 1935. It was then, in his first season as coach of the Southern Methodist Mustangs, that Bell produced what is still considered one of the greatest teams the Southwest has ever seen.

Bell, of course, has coached other good teams and has a reputation for consistently developing tricky, aerial-minded, dangerous elevens, but that 1935 machine, led by All-America Bobby Wilson, is the one they still talk about. Even his 1947 eleven, with All-America Doak Walker, unbeaten and tied once—and which gained Bell second place in the vote for Coach of the Year—would rank behind the achievement of 1935.

Bell's Mustangs, which won 12 and was tied once in '35, received the first invitation ever extended to a Southwest Conference team to participate in the Rose Bowl, and even after losing 7 to 0 in a valiant Pasadena battle against Stanford, were awarded the Knute Rockne Memorial Trophy emblematic of the National Football championship.

As a player for Centre's famous "Praying Colonels," Bell came close to All-America line recognition. He was a teammate of Bo McMillan, now coach of Indiana. Together they gained their football knowledge with one of the outstanding "little" teams in the history of football.

MATTY BELL
Southern Methodist 20, Texas Christian 14.
FORT WORTH, TEXAS, NOVEMBER 30, 1935.

This game is described by historians as a game that sent seasoned sportswriters such as Grantland Rice, and other notable knights of the pen, into hysterics that found an outlet in some of the finest football stories ever printed.

An invitation to the Rose Bowl—first to be received by any Southwest Conference team—depended on the outcome of the Southern Methodist-Texas Christian battle for the Conference championship on November 30, 1935. Both teams were undefeated, with a string of 10 victories each, and both were led by great All-Americas —the Mustangs by Bobby Wilson, and the Horned Frogs by Sammy Baugh; and this was my first season at Southern Methodist.

It was truly a battle of two great teams and it's difficult for me or anyone, partisan or otherwise, in that crowd of 40,000, to describe the feeling they experienced when with minutes remaining, fourth down and seven yards to go, Bob Finley passed 44 yards to Robert Wilson for the touchdown that gave us the game, 20 to 14.

Even in the dying moments, with Baugh's arm ever-cocked to throw those deadly, accurate passes, we never believed this ball game was quite won.

Baugh was in a passing mood—more so, than ever, that afternoon. When the smoke from his firing had lifted, the statistics showed that Sammy had heaved 43 forwards, completed 17 of them for 172 yards and one touchdown, and had only one intercepted. Our defense thought it was in a basketball game.

But we got away to a 14-0 lead. The first score came on a steady march in the opening period in which we bit off only two large chunks. These were a 12-yard pass from Wilson to Sprague, and a 17-yard off tackle slant by Burt. With the ball resting on TCU's one, Finley banged over the goal line and Orr converted.

In the second period, we started moving again from our 20. Little Wilson, the smallest man on the field and yet the best back, swept around end for 22 yards. Burt picked up three and Finley 18 before Finley hit Stewart with a long pass. Then, with the ball on the Horned Frog 14, Sprague lateraled to Wilson and Bobby tore around end for the touchdown. Orr's placekick made it 14 to 0.

Just when it looked as though we might have an easy time of it, Baugh got his mates into action. They took the kickoff, and, with Baugh, Jim Lawrence and Tillie Manton carrying, put the ball on our 22 before we knew what hit us. Then Sammy passed to Will Walls on the two, where it was ruled complete because of interference. Lawrence plunged over and Roach's point cut our lead in half.

There was no scoring in a fiercely battled third period. We were out to protect our lead and TCU, desperately trying to tie the score, could not break through despite Baugh's perfect passes, too many of which were dropped by overanxious receivers. It was different at the start of the fourth period.

The Horned Frogs weren't dropping any more. A run by Lawrence brought them deep into our territory, and then Baugh pitched to Walls, who brought it down to the eight. On the next play, Baugh found Lawrence with the touchdown throw. Roach kicked the point and the game we had started out to win early was now tied at 14-all with only eight minutes of play remaining.

An ordinary team would have cracked under the consistent drive of an opponent like TCU. The Mustangs, however, were not an ordinary team. Roach kicked off and Smith raced the ball back to our 40. Finley battered the line for four. Then Smith made it first down at midfield. We were gaining slowly and steadily, but time, too, was gaining. We called two more smashes but the Horned Frogs held us to three yards. It was fourth down, seven to go, and with the minutes speeding by only one way to travel—through the air.

Even in this "flying circus" of a game, I doubt if Texas Christian expected us to pass. We were on the 47, a long way from touchdown territory. An interception might mean the ball game for the Horned Frogs—an incomplete pass would give Baugh more time to whip that ball around.

The Ponies lined up in punt formation. Everything seemed normal for the routine, safe fourth down kick. Finley received the ball. Flawlessly, without wasting motion, he faked the punt. Suddenly, he faded back, and shooting down the field was Wilson. Sensing the drama of the daring play, the crowd stood up as one. As Wilson headed for the goal line, Finley let the ball go. If ever there was a man with a mission, a man with a will to get somewhere at the right time, it was the astounding Wilson. The ball sailed through the air, and Wilson raced with it, both outspeeding the secondary. Would they meet?

What elements combined to complete the next few seconds nobody but Wilson will ever know. Here was a man who seemed positive he would make that catch. Perhaps it was desperation mixed with a momentary super greatness—but as the ball came down Wilson stopped running. With perfect timing, he seemed to lift himself off the ground to snatch the ball—not by much—but he had it. The catch they later called the "$85,000 catch," was made on the seven-yard line. It was not over yet as three huge Horned Frogs stood between Wilson and the goal line. It would have been anti-climactic for Wilson to be stopped there, however. How he did it, doesn't matter. He got by those three tacklers and went over the goal line to the tumult of an ovation never before heard in the Southwest.

The Horned Frogs took the kickoff and fought those last minutes as few teams have ever fought before. With the gallant Baugh pitching, there was no letting up. Twice, as the seconds faded, he passed the Frogs into threatening positions. But the threats never materialized.

We went into the Rose Bowl and there was no disgrace in losing to Bobby Grayson's great Stanford team, 7 to 0. It was a tough one to lose, but I was proud of those 1935 Mustangs nonetheless, and as the Texas papers so aptly put it, "they wrote, with sparkling cleats, enough football history to make even their severest critics soon forget their failure in the Rose Bowl, a failure that well could be attributed to the letdown that invariably follows a strenuous and victorious season, plus the excitement of playing before one of the mightiest throngs ever to see two elevens in hand-to-hand combat anywhere." (The crowd was 85,000).

It served to emphasize my greatest day in football.

The lineup:

SOUTHERN METHODIST

(20)	pos.	TEXAS CHRISTIAN (14)
Tipton	le	Meyer
Spain	lt	Ellis
Wetzel	lg	Harrison
Johnson	c	Lester
Stamps	rg	Kellow
Orr	rt	Groseclose
Stewart	re	Roach
Sprague	qb	Baugh
Wilson	lh	Clark
Burt	rh	Lawrence
Turner	fb	Manton

Southern Methodist ....7—7—0—6——20
Texas Christian ....0—7—0—7——14

Touchdowns: *Southern Methodist*—Finley, Wilson, 2. *Texas Christian*—Lawrence, 2.

Points after touchdowns: *Southern Methodist*—Orr, 2. *Texas Christian*—Roach, 2.

Substitutions: *Southern Methodist*—Stufflebeme, Scottino, Raborn, Russell, Smith. *Texas Christian*—Walls, Diggs, Lenne, Rogers, Kline, McCall, McClure, Montgomery.

Referee—Curtis, Texas A & M. Head Linesman—Fouts, Baylor. Field Judge—Petty, Texas A & M.

DANA X. BIBLE

(Carson-Newman, '12)

BRANDON PREP, TENN., 1912.
MISSISSIPPI COLLEGE, 1913-1915.
LOUISIANA STATE, 1916.
TEXAS A & M, 1917-1928.
NEBRASKA, 1929-1936.
TEXAS, 1937-1946.

Thirty-four years of coaching football and helping to make its rules is an enviable record for any man.

Dana Bible called it a coaching day at the end of the 1946 season and decided to concentrate on being Athletic Director at Texas but he left behind him a brilliant mark of achievement on the nation's gridirons. His teams won 209 games, lost 64 and tied 19, including five Southwest Conference championships at Texas A & M, three at Texas, and five Big Six crowns at Nebraska. Three appearances in the Cotton Bowl with U. of Texas teams produced two victories and one tie.

Bible was a star athlete at Carson-Newman, where he partici-pated in football, track and baseball, and he moved quickly in the coaching field on graduation in 1912. It was at Texas A & M that Bible really hit the headlines. His 1917 first season team won eight, lost none, and scored 270 points without yielding one. In 1919, the Aggies won 10 in another undefeated and untied season and scored 275 points against nothing for the opposition. It wasn't until the annual Thanksgiving Day classic in 1920 with Texas that his team was beaten, 7 to 3.

Only twelve men represent the Collegiate Rules Committee throughout the nation and Bible has been a member for 22 years—quite a tribute to a man who has successfully devoted his lifetime to coaching.

DANA BIBLE
Texas A & M 22, Centre College 14.
DIXIE CLASSIC, DALLAS, TEXAS, JANUARY 1, 1922.

The record books for some strange reason do not show that the Dixie Classic was actually the second in the long parade of Bowl games. They don't mention this annual game, named after baseball's Dixie Classic, possibly because the Bowl tag didn't go with it but out of it blossomed what is now known as the Cotton Bowl.

The game in Dallas matched the winner of the Southwestern Conference champion with the top team in the old Southern Conference. The Dixie Classic which brought together Texas A & M and the famous Prayin' Colonels of Centre College on January 1, 1922, was as great a contest as any Bowl game ever produced. It certainly ranks with the great upsets in football history, for our Aggies defeated nationally-rated Centre, 22 to 14.

Centre College, a little school with an enrollment of 254 students in Danville, Ky., wasn't always famous. It was in 1919 that the nation first heard rumblings of a "Wonder Team." They won nine straight that year, scoring 485 points to 23 for the opposition. Coached by "Uncle Charlie" Moran, the former baseball umpire, they roared on in 1920 but fell before Harvard, 31 to 14, in a game called the greatest football ever played in the East up to that time.

They came back to Cambridge in 1921 and, led by Alvin (Bo) McMillin, stunned the football world by upsetting mighty Harvard,

Dana X. Bible (seated left) at the Football Rules Committee meeting at Palm Springs, Fla., 1936, with many football notables.

6 to 0—a Harvard eleven that had won 22 games in a row and had played three ties. It was then that Centre became famous. Up to that time, it had been nothing more than a college that had produced 26 college presidents, eight United States Senators, and 37 Congressmen.

The startling victory over Harvard made Centre the people's choice. They were hailed not only as a great team but as one of the best of all-time. This was the team which Texas A & M had to face in Dallas on New Year's Day.

Texas A & M was not a weak team but off the record neither was it an exceptionally strong one. We had no All-Americas like Bo McMillin or ends like Roberts and James. Their line molded by Claude (Tiny) Thornhill was a powerhouse which yielded only six points in 10 games. Centre, meanwhile, had scored 320 points in winning all 10 games. It was no wonder that the Colonels were figured a 20-point favorite.

Centre was confident that it would stretch a two-year winning streak to 15 games against us. This was supposed to be a honeymoon for them. In fact, McMillin had been married the night before the game and his bride sat on the Centre bench equally positive that the Kentuckians would romp right through us.

Puny Wilson and Heinie Weir had paced us to the Southwestern Conference title in 1921. They were our stalwarts to stop the predicted slaughter. Wilson got us the first break when he broke through to tackle fullback Bartlett for a safety. Bartlett had taken a punt behind his own goal line but Wilson's speed cut him down before he could get over.

The "breaks" were evened in the second quarter when Captain Weir was carried off the field with a broken leg.

With Weir out, that 2-0 lead we owned at the end of the half seemed meaningless. It was a battle of lines, a bruising, relentless fight. We had two great chances to score at the start of the second half. We flubbed both of them as Centre stopped us twice within the shadow of its goal line. They kicked out of danger but the punt was fumbled and Tanner recovered for Centre. Shortly afterward, the vaunted Colonel power showed itself. Snoddy bucked over for the game's first touchdown and as Roberts converted, our margin vanished. The expected rout of the Aggies seemed underway.

The crowd of 11,554, a record for the old Dixie Classic, sat up for the bombardment of Centre fireworks, but it was the Aggies who sparkled. We took the kickoff and pounded away at the Colonel line. Miller's long pass to Evans ended the march in a touchdown. I rushed in McMillan, not to be confused with Bo McMillin, and he converted to put us ahead, 9 to 7.

Not even the partisan Texas fans could believe that our heroic efforts were more than a flash in the Texas sun. The publicity attained by Centre had overawed all but the Aggies. Everyone waited for the Kentucky avalanche but once again it was Texas that struck with lightning speed and the fleet feet of Puny Wilson. Behind perfect interference, Wilson raced 30 yards to a score before the third period was over. McMillan's kick made it 16 to 7 and for the first time in the game, an upset loomed.

It was a desperate, overanxious Centre team that started the fourth quarter in an effort to overhaul the Aggies. Desperation, however, can produce disastrous results. McMillin, who never quite lived up to his All-America rating in the game, was hampered by a bad pass from center early in the period. He got off a wobbly pass that landed in the arms of the Aggies' Winn. Winn scored and though McMillin failed to convert, the 15-point margin seemed big enough.

With 10 minutes remaining, the Colonels tried every trick in the book. Finally, in the waning minutes, a tricky forward-lateral maneuver on which McMillin passed to Covington, who then lateraled to Snoddy, gave them their second touchdown. Roberts kicked the extra point but that in itself was a futile gesture. The mighty Prayin' Colonels of Centre were beaten.

We fought this game against terrific odds and the achievement of winning is still considered one of the greatest reversals of form in football history. Not our form, of course, for nobody except our own Aggie circle figured that anybody could dent the stonewall defenses and withstand the scoring onslaught of the little Kentucky college which had humbled great Harvard. This was not so much a game of thrills as of complete satisfaction to me because I had full faith in the ability of the Aggies. They gave me my greatest day in football.

The lineup:
TEXAS A & M

(22)	pos.	CENTRE (14)
Wilson	le	Roberts
Winn	lt	Gordy
Murrah	lg	Jones
Du Bois	c	Kubale
Dieterich	rg	Shadoens
Carruthers	rt	Cragor
Evans	re	James
Morris	qb	McMillin
Weir (C)	lh	Armstrong (C)
Sanders	rh	Snoddy
Miller	fb	Tanner

Texas A & M .... 2—0—14—6——22
Centre .... 0—0—7—7——14.

Touchdowns: *Texas A & M*—Evans, Wilson, Winn. *Centre*—Snoddy, 2.

Points after touchdowns: *Texas A & M*—McMillan, 2. *Centre*—Roberts, 2.

Safety: *Centre*—Bartlett.

Substitutions: *Texas A & M*—Beesley, McMillan, Johnson, Keen. *Centre*—Covington, Bartlett, Rubarth, Gibson, Bene, Lemon, Thomasson.

EARL (RED) BLAIK

(*U. S. Military Academy, '20*)
U. S. MILITARY ACADEMY, 1927-33.
DARTMOUTH, 1934-40.
U. S. MILITARY ACADEMY, 1941-

The young looking Earl Blaik started an extremely active athletic career in Ohio as an end on Dayton's Steele High School team. Two years later he was participating in Miami (O.) U.'s sports program as an end, outfielder and sprinter. He added a fourth sport, basketball, when he entered West Point in 1918.

Serving only two years, under an accelerated wartime setup, Blaik was commissioned in 1920. He retained his lieutenancy until 1923 when he resigned from the Army. He was persuaded to give up business and help his former Miami coach, George Little, with the Wisconsin ends.

From there Blaik moved to West Point as an end coach during the Biff Jones, Ralph Sasse and Gar Davidson regimes. He made such a fine mark that Dartmouth named him head coach in 1934.

There followed seven years helping the Big Green climb off the floor of the Ivy League. When, in 1940, Army's football fortunes hit rock bottom, Blaik answered the call for help.

In his first season, the Cadets won five, lost three and tied one— but that deadlock was a cherished scoreless tie with Notre Dame. The next campaign saw the revitalized West Pointers capture six contests and, by 1943, Blaik had substituted the T-formation and Glenn Davis to notch a 7-2-1 record.

From 1944, when Doc Blanchard joined Davis in forming the greatest one-two collegiate football punch in history, the Kaydets rolled unbeaten through three seasons. They recorded 27 straight victories, interrupted only by the 1946 scoreless battle with Notre Dame. And, in 1946, he was named Coach of the Year—a fitting tribute.

EARL BLAIK
Dartmouth 3, Cornell 0.
HANOVER, N. H., NOVEMBER 16, 1940.

Not only did my Dartmouth team of 1940 give me my greatest thrill by upsetting a powerful Cornell machine but it gave football one of its greatest games.

There are so many reasons why that particular game will live forever in gridiron history that I hardly know where to start. For its weird combination of circumstances, the contest probably never will be matched.

Imagine winning a football game TWO days after it was played. Yes, two days after we had dropped a 7-3 decision to undoubtedly Cornell's greatest team, we had it changed to a 3-0 victory for us. Historians rushed to their books trying to find a sequel to that one. The nearest thing discovered was an NYU-Columbia game played in 1922, which NYU apparently won, 7 to 6. A couple of days after the game, the referee ruled the NYU touchdown should have been a safety.

But NYU refused to recognize the decision, listing it as a 7-6 defeat of Columbia, while the Lions recorded it as a 6-2 defeat of the Violets. Our game, however, was conceded to us as a victory by Cornell—a rare case in which a team, scoring a tremendously important victory on a controversial play, officially reversed the decision when the mistake was recognized, a tribute to the Cornell officials and those who worked the football game.

Actually, the situation was a controversy within a controversy. Or a mistake within a mistake. And the post-game fireworks mushroomed into national prominence in view of other circumstances surrounding the battle.

Cornell was the No. 1 team in the nation. It had just defeated a powerful Ohio State eleven; had an 18-game winning streak and hadn't been beaten since 1938. Carl Snavely had substantially the same squad that had whipped us, 35 to 0, in 1939 and there wasn't much difference in our personnel, either.

In view of that, Cornell, it was figured, would surely beat us by 30 or 40 points. That's what everybody expected. Even the newspapers didn't bother sending their top writers, relying on student correspondents to cover them.

We worked on defense, primarily, and that's what won the

Earl Blaik, Army, and Frank Leahy, Notre Dame, talk things over before final Cadet-Irish battle.

game for us. Our six complicated defenses helped us turn the trick, with the aid of a tricky deviation. In lining up on defense, we placed our linemen one yard further back than usual. That extra yard off the line of scrimmage completely confused Cornell and upset its blocking assignments and precision.

Through the first half, the Big Red machine sputtered and backfired. It never got past midfield until the third quarter, while we were in their territory all the time . . . once giving up the ball on the six.

Cornell's first serious bid, in the third quarter, failed on our 17. Then end Bob Krieger gave Dartmouth a 3-0 lead by kicking an early fourth quarter field goal from the Cornell 27. It was quite a boot, in view of the slippery footing caused by a light snowfall, and served to send the Big Red into a fighting fury.

Cornell ripped to our 43, but Wolfe stopped the drive with a pass interception. Back they came to our eight where, once again, a pass was intercepted—this one by Kast. With two and a half minutes to play, Cornell started the march that led to the famous Fifth Down incident.

A flurry of passes brought first downs on our 41, 31, 18 and six.

Then came the much-discussed series of plays in the remaining minute. Here's how it happened:

(1) Mort Landsberg drove for three yards to the three.

(2) 45 seconds left and Walt Scholl made two to the one.

(3) 20 seconds remaining and Landsberg smashed center to about a foot short of the goal line.

(4) 10 seconds left and Coach Snavely sent in a sub to stop the clock, Cornell taking a five-yard penalty for excessive times out. Then Scholl tossed into the end zone where Hall, figuring it was fourth down, batted down a pass he might have intercepted.

(5) Referee Red Friesell, after starting to put the ball down on the 20, where it would belong to Dartmouth, changed his mind and placed it on our five. He signalled it was fourth down for Cornell coming up. Our captain and guard, Lou Young, protested vehemently, but Cornell was allowed to put the ball in play with three seconds left. On "fifth down," Scholl flipped a touchdown pass to halfback Bill Murphy.

All was confusion, and our kids were boiling mad. They stormed off the field and into my office still dressed in their uniforms. I advised them to be calm, telling them I had implicit faith in the officials. Yet, I had a hard time trying to figure out the thing.

There seemed to be only one possible explanation for Friesell's decision—both teams had incurred penalties on the fourth down, thus nullifying the play. Snavely, it was said later, thought there'd been a double-offside. We got to believing it just was another one of those unlucky breaks that had dogged us in a season wherein we lost to a Franklin & Marshall touchdown in the last minute; dropped a heart-breaking decision to Yale on practically the game's last play and saw Princeton beat us with only three minutes remaining.

My boys wanted to go and talk to the officials. But I assured them I'd straighten it out. It was about 10 or 15 minutes after we'd left the field when I went to see Friesell. He immediately told me that he had made a mistake and felt terrible about the whole thing.

Friesell was so hurt by his error that Dartmouth president Ernest Hawkins, and I, had a difficult time consoling him. We drove Red to the station and, throughout the ride, he kept giving himself verbal kicks in the pants for booting such an important decision. He told us that he didn't know exactly what good it would do, but he was going to admit his error in a report to Asa Bushnell, who was in charge of officials' assignments in the East.

Meanwhile the little town of Hanover was in an uproar. Everybody started yelling and parading from the moment the final gun sounded. There were bonfires and speeches. The players and I were forced to speak and we were treated like "conquering heroes." Unofficial protests hit every paper throughout the land, but in Hanover we were the winners. You couldn't convince those wild-cheering students and townsfolk otherwise. Maybe they anticipated what was coming.

Anyway, through Saturday night, Sunday and into Monday the "victory celebration" continued. It was while I was preparing to join the boys for Monday afternoon practice that the phone rang in my office. It was President Hawkins. He said:

"Earl, I just received word from President Rufus Day of Cornell. They agree they had a fifth down and concur that the score should have been 3-0 in Dartmouth's favor."

Snavely, after examining movies and all reports of the game, discussed the matter with President Day who, incidentally, was a

Dartmouth graduate. They decided to give us a 3 to 0 victory because the controversial play actually was the last of the game.

By the time I walked onto the practice field to tell the players, they'd already received the news through the grapevine. There was an appreciative reaction, anyway, when I gave it to them officially. Then they buckled down for the next game, thrilled, naturally, but unaware that I'd just been provided with my greatest thrill.

The lineup:

DARTMOUTH (3)	pos.	CORNELL (0)
Krieger	le	Schmuck
Crego	lt	Van Orden
Young	lg	Dunbar
Pearson	c	Finneran
Dacey	rg	Conti
Winship	rt	Drahos
J. Kelley	re	A. Kelley
Norton	qb	Matuszczak
Wolfe	lh	McCullough
Kast	rh	Murphy
Hall	fb	Landsberg

Cornell . . . . 0—0—0—0——0
Dartmouth . . . . 0—0—0—3——3

Field goal: *Dartmouth*—Krieger.

Substitutions: *Cornell*—Hersey, West, Jenkins, Hipolit, Scholl, Bufalino, Bohrman. *Dartmouth*—Gerber, Hickey, Crowley, Arico.

Referee—W. H. Friesell, Princeton. Umpire—W. R. Crowley, Bowdoin. Field judge—H. C. Haines, Penn State. Head Linesman—Joe McKenney, Boston College.

LT. FELIX A. (DOC) BLANCHARD
(*U. S. Military Academy, '47*)

Every year, the Amateur Athletic Union (AAU) votes the Sullivan Award to America's top athlete from a competitive and sportsmanlike viewpoint. Doc Blanchard, then a 20-year-old product of Bishopville, S. C., received it in 1945.

One of the select few in the history of the Military Academy who never was on a losing football team, the bone-crushing fullback was unanimous All-America choice in 1945 and 1946. From the time he made his first appearance in 1944 until the last 1946 game against Navy, Blanchard formed one of the most explosive football combinations ever known with Glenn Davis. They, Blanchard (Mr. Inside) and Davis (Mr. Outside), paced three Army teams through 28 unbeaten games, being tied by Notre Dame in 1946.

Along the glory road, Doc picked up the Heisman Memorial Award, the Maxwell Trophy, the Walter Camp Trophy and, of course, the aforementioned Sullivan Award. He gave some of his time to track and field activities as a weight man but did most of his damage for Army on the gridiron.

Son of a famous football star at Tulane and Wake Forest, Doc attended St. Stanislaus Prep School before engaging in a year of freshman football at North Carolina. His appointment to West Point came at a time while he was serving as an enlisted man in the regular Army. At the Academy, Doc's powerful line bursts from the T-formation, punting and great defensive play earned him immediate stardom as a plebe in 1944.

In 1945, Doc led the Army team in scoring with 19 touchdowns and one extra point. Injuries failed to nail down Blanchard in 1946 and he added nine touchdowns and two extra points to his total, despite being forced to the bench for a couple of games. He graduated from West Point in three years, under the accelerated, wartime program.

LT. DOC BLANCHARD
Army 59, Notre Dame 0.
NEW YORK, NOVEMBER 11, 1944.

Offhand, as I look back, some of the things I remember best are the 92-yard kickoff return I made in the 1946 game against Columbia; receiving the 1945 Sullivan Award; scoring my first Army touchdown; and being a part of West Point's Golden Era of Football.

Because of the combination of circumstances, however, I'd have to single out the 1944 game with Notre Dame as my greatest day.

Coach Earl Blaik has been criticized repeatedly for piling it on in that game. But I want to say right here and now that there isn't a semblance of truth in such charges. Actually, the first team played only 20 minutes. It simply was a case of everything we did being right while all Notre Dame tried to do was wrong.

Remember, before we played the game there were many who thought the Fighting Irish were the better team. They had potential All-Americas like Bob Kelly, Tree Adams, Pat Filley, Fred Rovai and Boley Dancewicz. On paper, they looked as good as we did. But there was one important thing in our favor—we had every traditional incentive working for us.

You see, this was more than just a game with Notre Dame. For 13 years the Irish had kept Army from winning. And, to inspire us further, we hadn't scored a point on Notre Dame in five years. Thus, Coach Blaik didn't have to spend any time "getting us up" for this

Felix (Doc) Blanchard, West Point's famous 35, goes wide to register gain against Pennsylvania.

game. In fact, now that I think of it, if anybody's to blame for the big score it's Notre Dame. Yes, Notre Dame, which fired our burning desire to win with its long humiliation of Army players.

We were the hungry fellows. Not Coach Blaik. Just the first team, second team and every player on the bench. We wanted this game and wanted it badly. We were a fighting fury as we lined up for the kickoff and our pent-up emotions were exploded like an atom bomb by the sound of the opening whistle. We were the fellows carrying the banner for Army teams that had failed to whip Notre Dame in 13 years.

I guess you can liken our furious will to win to that of a fighter; a fighter who has a grudge to settle and goes out to win by a knock-out. You might say we had the "killer instinct" in us that day, right down to the last man. And we . . . I and every fellow who got into the game . . . gave vent to that tremendous victory urge welled up within us by Notre Dame's prolonged mastery in the series.

As I said, we hadn't scored a point on the Irish in five years. We took care of that, but real quick. We got our hands on the ball three times at the very start of the game and Notre Dame was hit by the fastest three touchdowns it had seen or ever will see. Ten minutes and we had 20 points.

Two of the eight interceptions we pulled off during the game led to a pair of the first period touchdowns. Doug Kenna scored the first on a six-yard sprint at the end of a 44-yard drive. Then Kenna intercepted a Dancewicz pass on Notre Dame's 26. He faked an aerial to Glenn Davis and handed off to speedy Max Minor for our second touchdown.

It was Kenna, once again, after I intercepted another Dancewicz pass on the Notre Dame 35. Doug stepped right back and flipped a touchdown aerial to Ed Rafalko. So, at the end of the first period, we owned a 20-0 lead and Notre Dame hadn't scored even a first down against our fierce-charging Tex Coulter, Barney Poole, Hank Foldberg, Al Nemetz, Dick Pitzer, Bob St. Onge, etc.

I don't know what people, who've criticized us since, would've had us do at that point. Maybe if we were sure at the time that the 20-0 lead would be sufficient we might've stopped. But there's no first period lead safe in the hopped-up football played these days, particularly against Notre Dame. So we went about our business of playing football.

Blanchard and Davis, Army's immortal Touchdown Twins.

On the first play of the second period, Davis set up the first of his three touchdowns by intercepting a pass and racing 47 yards to Notre Dame's six. Lombardo immediately handed the ball to Davis, who streaked around right end without being touched.

Shortly, thereafter, a freak accident occurred that helped add to the unforgettable moments of this game. I took a T-formation handoff and headed around end behind my interference. I recall, only, brushing past a couple of fellows on my way to a short gain, but after getting to my feet I saw some of the players huddled around an official.

To this day, you can't prove it by me that I crashed into Head Linesman Dave Reese. But the players said I did, the newspapermen said I did, so I must've been the fellow who unconsciously ran into Mr. Reese and put him out of the game with a dislocated elbow. It was an embarrassing situation because Mr. Reese and I were pretty friendly.

Anyway, play was resumed with the insertion of a sub Head Linesman and we took up the scoring where we left off a little later. Behind beautiful blocking, Kenna grabbed Kelly's punt, reversed his field and raced 34 yards to Notre Dame's 21. Davis followed with his second touchdown, another dash around right end from the six. It now was, 33 to 0, and only the first half gone.

There was no stopping us, though. Everything worked for us, no matter whether it was the first or second team playing. Notre Dame's fine bunch of players just didn't have the stuff to match us. They were truly Fighting Irish, never giving up, but you couldn't beat the Army that day with just heart. Minor showed why when Kenna started to his right and reversed the ball to the speedy half-back, who opened the second half with a 60-yard touchdown trip down the sidelines.

Again it was Kenna as Army got touchdown No. 7. After Kelly's fumble was recovered on Notre Dame's 16, Doug passed six yards to Pitzer for the score.

The last period was marked by Davis' third touchdown—a 55-yard sprint through tackle on a fake pass play—and five pass interceptions. The last aerial steal was a goal-line, touchdown stab of a Joe Gasparella heave by Hal Tavzel, an "obscure tackle," as the newspapers called him the next day, and his wild reaction indicated the spirit which kept Army driving all afternoon. This "obscure tackle," scoring a needless touchdown, the last of a 59-0 victory, waved his hands crazily, jumped up and down like a kid on a pogo stick and yelled in mad glee. It took the fellows on the field a few minutes to quiet Tavzel, who acted as though he had just scored the winning touchdown.

Our two teams and the third stringers who played were terrific. They held the Irish to 70 yards gained and completely bottled up Kelly, who, out of fairness, was hobbled some by a leg injury. It all added up to Notre Dame's worst defeat in its long football history; one that probably never will be matched.

(Ed. Note—Army's two teams were terrific, but so was Blanchard. Here's a newspaper excerpt from a story of the game):

"None were more conspicuous in the victory than was Felix (Doc) Blanchard, the powerful plebe fullback. It was Blanchard who sent kickoffs into the end zone, who punted when Kenna was not on the field, who intercepted passes and was even more poisonous on the defense than he was carrying the ball."

The lineup:

ARMY (59)	pos.	NOTRE DAME (0)
Pitzer	le	O'Connor
Arnold	lt	Sullivan
Green	lg	Filley
St. Onge	c	Szymanski
Stanowicz	rg	Rovai
Nemetz	rt	Adams
Rafalko	re	Guthrie
Kenna	qb	Dancewicz
Hall	lh	Marino
Minor	rh	Kelly
Blanchard	fb	Angsman

Army ....20—13—13—13——59
Notre Dame ....0—0—0—0——0

Touchdowns: *Army*—Davis 3, Minor 2, Kenna, Rafalko, Pitzer, Tavzel.

Points after touchdowns: *Army*—Walterhouse 5.

Substitutions: *Army*—Poole, Foldberg, T. Hayes, Wayne, Halligan, Webb, Coulter, Gelini, LaMar, Tavzel, R. Hayes, Yancey, Biles, Gerometta, Enos, Fuson, Bresnehan, Lake, Lombardo, Sensanbaugher, Walterhouse, Davis, Dobbs, Tucker, Chabot, West, Sauer. *Notre Dame*—Westenkirchner, Marty,

Berezney, J. Kelly, Schuster, Mergenthal, Ganey, Dailer, Mastrangelo, Stewart, Ray, Nemeth, Chandler, Gasparella, Fitsgerald, Wendell, Corbiseno, Lebrau.

Referee—Dave Nobel, Nebraska. Umpire—E. C. Krieger, Ohio U. Field Judge—Rollie Barnum, Wisconsin. Head Linesman —Dave Reese, Denison.

PAUL BROWN
(Miami, O., '30)
SEVERN PREP, 1930-1931.
MASSILLON HIGH SCHOOL, 1932-1940.
OHIO STATE, 1941-1943.
CLEVELAND BROWNS, 1946-   .

In 1940, Paul Brown was coaching a high school football team in Massillon, Ohio. In 1946, the same Paul Brown was hailed as the outstanding coach in professional football. His Cleveland Browns had won the first All-America Conference championship. To prove that it wasn't an accident, the Browns did it again in 1947.

A sound fundamentalist, Brown first attracted nationwide attention when he coached Massillon High to six straight Ohio championships. A 120-pound frame had handicapped his own football ambitions and caused him to switch from Ohio State in favor of Miami University at Oxford, Ohio. In 1941, Brown returned to Ohio State —as head football coach replacing Francis Schmidt.

Football thrived at Ohio State under Brown. He started with a 6-1-1 record and in 1942 led them to the Big Ten crown and the national championship with nine triumphs and one defeat. The war wrecked his 1943 eleven and the following year he himself went into the Navy. He coached the Great Lakes team for two years, including among his triumphs a 39-7 upset of Notre Dame.

Returning to civilian life, Brown signed to coach Cleveland in the newly-formed All-America Conference. This comparatively young coach—he is under the 40-year mark—has risen more rapidly on the football horizon than possibly any other coach. Brown of the Browns will be heard from for many years to come.

PAUL BROWN
Massillon High 6, Canton High 0.
CANTON, O., NOVEMBER 23, 1935.

Many years ago professional football was cradled in the Canton-Massillon area and the grudge battles between the Canton Bulldogs and the Massillon Agathons were bitterly fought affairs. The National Football League had its birth in this region and it was inevitable that the rivalry should be shared by the high school teams of Canton McKinley and Massillon Washington.

That November afternoon in 1935 was an important one for Massillon fans; but more so for me. In 1932 I had accepted the job of coaching Massillon, where I was quarterback in my undergraduate days. Three years in a row, Coach Jimmy Aiken's teams had beaten us. Never had a Massillon junior or senior high school football team whipped the Bulldogs on their Lehman Field, now we were on the verge of our first unbeaten season since 1922 and were seeking our first county championship in 11 years, the first state title in 13.

For miles around fans flocked to see this traditional rivalry in its 25th renewal. About 4000 unreserved seats were placed on sale at 11 a.m. the day of the game and there were double that number of people on hand before the windows opened. Some 12,000 packed the stands by game-time, with thousands turned away. Most of the crowd was Massillon rooters who had traveled over to cheer us on to our 14th series victory—Canton having won nine, with two ties.

We were strong favorites despite the fact we had to pick a team from a student enrollment of 1100 as compared to Canton's 5000.

We had allowed 13 points while scoring 477. Canton had proved easy to score on so every psychological advantage was on our side.

Nine of our starting boys had never beaten Canton and were playing their last game. Capt. Augie Morningstar, Eddie Molinski, Neri Buggs and Howie Dutton had tasted defeat three years in a row. They were so bitterly inspired that they promised:

"We'll beat Canton or be carried off the field."

They were carried off the field, all right, but as winners—of one of the hardest-fought games I'll ever witness. From the start the elements conspired against us. With the fall of rain, we were forced to temper our wide-open attack and practically discard the forward pass which had been one of our most potent weapons.

The slippery field helped even matters, with the result that only one touchdown was scored that afternoon. Fortunately we got it. And the margin of difference was provided by a wonderful kid, Bob Glass, who went from stardom at Tulane into a World War II uniform and died a hero's death on Iwo Jima. The fans who saw the bitterly contested football game will never forget Glass.

We started as though we were going to make a rout of the game, only to quickly discover that the Bulldogs were super-charged almost beyond belief. After sloshing and sliding around the field on a long drive, Jake Gillom was stopped inches from a touchdown on a tackle slant by the determined Canton youngsters. That was in the opening minutes of the game.

Having been halted like that, we became conservative—maybe too conservative. We stuck to straight football in the hopes of getting a break. We figured we could keep Canton from scoring so all we had to do was wait for our opportunity. One period passed and no score. A second period passed and still no score. Then it came, the break we had been playing and praying for. Canton's Ray Sabin, one of the fastest men on the field, committed his team's only fumble early in the second half and we had our chance when Charley Anderson recovered on the Bulldog 21. You could sense that our kids knew this was the opportunity to win. And the fury with which they drove that 21 yards for a touchdown proved it.

Gillom raced three yards around right end—Gillom is now my ace kicker with the Cleveland Browns. Then Dutton ducked over right tackle to the 16. It was up to Glass, now, our fullback, who had carried only four times previously.

Glass powered through for a first down on the 11. Dutton again called on Glass for a line smash which moved the ball forward for four more precious yards. With the defense set for Glass, Dutton crossed 'em up by pounding left tackle to the five. Then Glass to the three and, on fourth down, Bobby blasted through center on a simple power play that produced the game's only touchdown. We were satisfied that we had victory in the bag, but not Canton. Big Don Scott, who later became an All-America lineman at Ohio State, smashed through to block Dutton's fourth down kick in the third period and recovered on our 25. Then Bill Adams passed to Jack Young for a first down on the six.

We immediately shifted into an eight-man line designed for goal-line situations. We were vulnerable, of course, to forward passes but counted on (1) the wet elements and (2) the hope that Canton wouldn't throw the ball from so close.

Sure enough, Canton tried to pierce our forward wall. Sabin made nothing off tackle and Adams was dumped for no gain trying to get around left end. As the fourth quarter started, Sabin was dropped for a yard loss on the seven. Now we knew a pass was coming and we rushed Danny Risoliti into a hurried heave that whizzed incomplete. That did it. Our victory was assured, although the Bulldogs did get to our 30 late in the game. But no further. Now you understand why that was and still is my greatest day in football.

The lineup:
MASSILLON
(6)	pos.	CANTON (0)
Anderson	le	Schultz
Held	lt	Scott
McDew	lg	Angelo
Voss	c	Rice
Woods	rg	Virdo
Buggs	rt	Wertman
Morningstar	re	Young
Dutton	qb	Risoliti
Gillom	lh	Sabin
Molinski	rh	Adams
Glass	fb	Ballos

Massillon .... 0—0—6—0——6
Canton .... 0—0—0—0——0
Touchdown: *Massillon*—Glass.

JAMES WALLACE (WALLY) BUTTS

(*Mercer, '29*)

MADISON A & M COLLEGE OF GEORGIA, 1929-1932.
GEORGIA MILITARY COLLEGE, 1933-1935.
MALE HIGH SCHOOL OF LOUISVILLE, KY., 1936-1937.
GEORGIA, 1938-   .

Wally Butts is one of the youngest and most successful head coaches in the college football ranks. The 43-year-old Georgia product has compiled a great record of having led five of his 10 Georgia teams into New Year's Day Bowl games. The Bulldogs never had a Bowl representative prior to his regime.

Butts came to Georgia as an assistant coach in 1938. The following year he was named to replace Harry Mehre as head coach. After two lean years in which he won 10, lost nine and tied one, Butts has kept the Bulldogs continually in the national spotlight. He has produced such great players as Frank Sinkwich, Charley Trippi and George Poschner. Trippi paced the 1946 team to Georgia's only unbeaten record under Butts—10 victories and no ties.

Noted for his conditioning tactics and some of the fanciest passing maneuvers in the nation, the former All-Southern end has been highly successful in his Bowl games. Only a 21-21 tie with Maryland in the Delta Bowl of January 1, 1948, mars the all-victory string of the Bulldogs. They whipped Texas Christian, 40 to 26, in the 1942 Orange Bowl, topped UCLA, 9 to 0, in the 1943 Rose Bowl, turned back Tulsa, 20 to 6, in the 1946 Oil Bowl, and tripped North Carolina, 20 to 10, in the 1947 Sugar Bowl.

An excellent after-dinner speaker as well as a "Bowl" authority, Butts has become a Georgia byword.

WALLY BUTTS
Georgia 21, Alabama 10.
ATLANTA, GA., OCTOBER 31, 1942.

I fought my way through the yelling, swirling crowd. All around me, people were shouting, "Nice game, Wally." . . . "Congratulations, Wally." . . . "Atta boy, Wally." Others were pounding me on the back, grabbing at my hand and jostling me so that my hat bounced off my head and almost got trampled.

I can't recall when fans reacted as wildly over a football game as did those Georgia rooters that day. They were hounding me as though I had just defeated a great Alabama team all by myself. I, in turn, was trying my darndest to claw my way into our dressing room. I wanted to do some congratulating of my own. I was burning with the same jubilant desire to slap my kids on their backs and cry: "Great game, Frankie" . . . "Swell, Georgie" . . .

How I ever made the locker room I'll never know. If I thought I had been in the middle of bedlam outside, you should've seen the inside. The Bulldogs filled the sweaty, crowded room with victory yells and songs. It was just one mad, happy scene and I did what any normal man would do under those joyful circumstances . . . I cried.

I cried tears of happiness. Tears of which I was proud. And as the reporters crowded around me and fired questions like an insurance doctor, all I could gasp was:

"I don't know what to say."

Even now, there isn't much to say other than, in my opinion, we had seen the greatest comeback a Georgia team ever made under my coaching. It certainly was the biggest thrill I have had in a coaching career of 19 years.

Nineteen years and nothing I've seen has ever matched the 21-10 victory over Alabama achieved by a potentially great Georgia team. Not just the victory itself, but how we did it.

But I'm far ahead of myself. There's more to the story than personal elation. In fact, it's a story of a fine group of American kids who didn't know the meaning of the word defeat.

Georgie Poschner was one of the main reasons why Georgia came from behind a 10-0 deficit in the last quarter that day to beat the highly favored Crimson Tide. Poschner's name won't be found in the All-America lists of 1942—although he did get honorable mention—but in my book he ranks with the great all-time ends. In fact, of that 1942 team, you'll find three names—Poschner at end, Sinkwich, at left halfback, and Ruark at guard, listed with all-time team in Georgia football history.

It was Poschner who caught two fourth-quarter touchdown passes from his Youngstown (Ohio) High School teammate Frankie Sinkwich. That was all Georgia needed to end Alabama's unbeaten streak and stretch its own to 12, atoning for the last Bulldog loss, which had been inflicted by the Crimson Tide. Before Poschner and Sinkwich delivered, however, it looked for a long time as though 'Bama would repeat its 1941 victory. The Crimson Tide rolled over us from the start. Its tough line, headed by Don Whitmire, who later starred at Navy, rode us off the field in the first period. It's amazing even now that we were able to hold them to only one first half touchdown—Russ Craft's cutback through his right tackle for a 47-yard touchdown run.

Faced with that quick deficit, we gambled at every opportunity in an attempt to catch up. Sinkwich, whose passing we'd hoped would more than make up for Alabama's pre-game edge in the line, tossed pass after pass. We even had Frankie try three from our end zone, after Russ Mosley had kicked out on our six just before the end of the first half. The first two daring aerials fell incomplete, but the third was taken by fullback Dick McPhee almost on the goal line and brought out to the 22.

Sinkwich then heaved to Van Davis on the 35, where a roughing penalty put the ball at midfield. With seconds left, I rushed in Charley Trippi with a pass play that ended in an interception by Mosley as the halftime gun sounded. We were lucky 'Bama hadn't scored on that interception. Thus we trailed by 7 to 0.

When Hecht, who had kicked Alabama's extra point, booted a 30-yard field goal in the third period, we became desperate. I sent out instructions to "Shoot the works" and Sinkwich did. He threw the ball all over the lot and began connecting.

After the 'Bama field goal put us behind, 10 to 0, we put the ball in play on our 22. As the game moved into the last quarter, Sinkwich alternated passes to end Van Davis and wingback Lamar Davis. Four first downs and we were on Alabama's 10. Frankie altered the throwing pattern with a five-yard smash over right tackle and then fired a bullet to Poschner for the touchdown.

Leo Costa's first of three conversions made it 10 to 7. And Alabama, sensing an aroused Bulldog, went into a defensive shell after taking the kickoff. A beautiful quick-kick by Mosley was downed on our 31. They thought they had us cooled off and beaten. But they didn't know Sinkwich, Poschner and the rest of our gallant kids.

Sinkwich handled the ball in seven of the eight plays that followed. Five were passes, four going to the Davis boys and the pay-off pitch to Poschner. Costa put us ahead, 14 to 10, and now it was Alabama's turn to fight back.

That it tried to do, after our kickoff gave the Tide the ball on its 45. But our linemen never gave them a chance. Mosley was downed for a five-yard loss trying to pass and a holding penalty put Alabama back on its 25. Mosley then tried to cross us up with a slash off tackle, only to be hit so hard he fumbled. The ball was picked out of the air by Dudish and carried for a needless but clinching touchdown.

That was the wind-up of a great team triumph and, also, a personal one for Poschner and Sinkwich. Although Frankie was held to but 36 yards in 20 running attempts, he threw 33 of Georgia's 37 passes and completed 17 for 230 yards.

It was that victory over Alabama which put Georgia into the New Year's Day Rose Bowl for the first time. Despite a 27-13 defeat by Auburn in our next to last game, we closed with a 34-0 swamping of Georgia Tech and then went out to Pasadena for a 9-0 whipping of UCLA.

There is a sadness to this—my greatest day in football—because the same Poschner who made those leaping, daring catches came out of the war with both legs shot off. I'll never forget the game nor the great, game kid who made that victory possible.

The lineup:

GEORGIA (21) pos.		ALABAMA (10)
Poschner	le	Sharp
Ellenson	lt	Whitmire
Miller	lg	Hecht
Godwin	c	Domnanovich
Ruark	rg	Leon
Williams	rt	Olenski
V. Davis	re	Weeks
Keuper	qb	Sabb
Sinkwich	lh	Mosley
L. Davis	rh	Craft
McPhee	fb	Salle

Georgia .... 0—0—0—21——21
Alabama .... 7—0—3—0——10

Touchdowns: *Georgia*—Poschner, 2, Dudish. *Alabama*—Craft.
Points after touchdowns: *Georgia*—Costa, 3. *Alabama*—Hecht.
Field goal: *Alabama*—Hecht.
Substitutions: *Georgia*—Tereshinski, King, Strother, J. Pierce, Boyd, Kumansky, Lee, Ehrhardt, Trippi, Dudish, Maguire, Todd, Nunnally. *Alabama*—Roberts, Leeth, Cook, Fishman, McKeeven, Compton, McCosky, Staples, Baughman, McWhorter, August, Brown, Reese, Scales, Jenkins.

FRANK CARIDEO

(Notre Dame, '31)

PURDUE, 1931.
MISSOURI, 1932-1934.
MISSISSIPPI STATE, 1935-1938.
IOWA, 1939-1942, 1946- .

"A rapier with brains in the hilt."

That's what they called Frank Carideo, and they couldn't have selected a better description for the quarterback of two of Notre Dame's greatest teams—the last two ever coached by the immortal Knute Rockne.

It was in 1929 and 1930 that Carideo masterminded the Irish through two successive undefeated and untied seasons, undisputed National Championships—and for himself, All-America honors each year. Rockne had called the 1930 team the greatest he ever coached, a tremendous tribute from the man who had produced truly mighty football machines.

In addition to being a superb signal-caller with an uncanny, almost psychic ability to pick the right play at the proper time, Carideo was an excellent passer, punter and blocker, and on occasion, a brilliant runner. He scored touchdowns in 1929 on runs of 75, 65 and 85 yards.

Carideo was also a member of the ordinary but inspired Rambler team of 1928 which went out and won the Army game "For the Gipper" after a soul-stirring historic dressing room appeal from Rockne.

Three quarterbacks stand out in Notre Dame's victory-studded history in the Rockne era—Gus Dorais, Harry Stuhldreher, and last, but far from the proverbial least, Frank Carideo.

FRANK CARIDEO
Notre Dame 14, Northwestern 0.
EVANSTON, ILL., NOVEMBER 22, 1930.

When you've played under Knute Rockne and felt the mighty magic of his teaching both practical and inspirational, it is easy to confuse the word "thrill" with "my greatest day." The selection between them becomes even more difficult when the immortal football master also happened to call the team you've played on the greatest he ever coached. When you consider that Rockne coached not only some of the finest gridiron machines in the history of football, and such players as George Gipp, The Four Horsemen, The Seven Mules, among others, the tribute seems almost frightening. That, I will never forget, nor the fact that I played on the last eleven Rockne coached before untimely death reached out and claimed him.

There was, however, what I consider a "great day"—the outstanding memory of my playing days with such unequalled teammates as Jack Elder, Marchy Schwartz, Marty Brill, "Jumping Joe" Savoldi, Larry "Moon" Mullins, Bucky O'Connor, Jack Cannon, Bert Metzger, John Law, Tom Yarr, Tom Conley, Frank Leahy, and other members of the Fighting Irish. Together, we went through 19 unbeaten and untied games.

The day I call outstanding is the one on which we played Northwestern's Wildcats at Evanston in 1930. It was the traditional game between the two teams and it sticks in my mind because of the very fortunate feat accomplished through the teaching given me by the late Leroy Mills regarding the kicking department.

The game was played on a perfect Fall day and brought together two undefeated records. Northwestern had already completed its Big Ten schedule as champion. This game against us would give them undisputed claim to the national crown—if they won it, which meant stopping our 17 game winning streak.

I've played in a lot of games but I can recall none as tough and as hard as this one turned out to be. The first half ended scoreless. Northwestern had made considerably more yardage than Notre Dame; in fact they had been on our goal line at least twice during that half. In the third quarter and the early part of the final period, Northwestern still seemed to hold the edge. Still, no score, as the Irish line held grimly. It was in that fourth quarter that the bitter struggle turned into a memorable one for me.

With four and a half minutes left in the ball game and Notre Dame's ball in the middle of the field, I proceeded to kick on first down. I did this with one hope—if I could kick out of bounds inside the five-yard line, it would force them to kick back and there might be a possibility of blocking their kick to break the deadlock. The kick went out on the half-yard line. I kicked three more first down punts out inside the one-yard marker. To be exact, two went out on the half-yard line, and one went out on the one-yard line. Those were "breaks" but we weren't able to block any of their return kicks.

It was on their last kick-out that our efforts brought reward. I caught their punt on the 50 and carried it back to the 28. This all happened with two minutes of play left. It was now first down for the Irish and 10 to go on the Wildcat 28. Instead of lining up in punt formation, we went into the Notre Dame shift and ran a reverse play with Marchy Schwartz running for a touchdown. We kicked the point and it was 7 to 0.

A desperate Northwestern team tried valiantly to crack through the Irish defense but we held them. Their kick from the 20 was weak and we returned it to the 30, with only a series of plays remaining. A sequence of Schwartz reverses ended up in a pass to me out in the flat and put the ball down on the half-yard line. Then one of our sophomore fullbacks, Dick Hanley, plunged it over for the second touchdown. I was successful with the extra point and it was 14 to 0.

From the above story, you can see it was quite a memorable

afternoon, inasmuch as Northwestern outplayed Notre Dame for 55½ minutes before I resorted to the kicking game to get a score. Mind you, there were only four and a half minutes left in the ball game when I elected to kick four consecutive punts on first down and had all of them go out inside the one-yard line.

This, I feel, broke their morale, and they let up just enough for us to get the vital first score—and then the ball game was over.

The power that was Northwestern's can be seen in the fact that five of the Wildcats—Woodworth, Baker, Marvil, Bruder and Russell—were not only prominently mentioned for All-America honors but were selected for All-Time recognition in Northwestern football annals.

The lineup:

NOTRE DAME (14)	pos.	NORTHWESTERN (0)
Host	le	Baker
Culver	lt	Engebritsen
Kassis	lg	Woodworth
Yarr	c	Clark
Metzger	rg	Evans
Kurth	rt	Marvil
Conley	re	Finol
Carideo	qb	Leach
Schwartz	lh	Bruder
Brill	rh	L. Hanley
Mullins	fb	Russell

Notre Dame . . . . 0—0—0—14——14
Northwestern . . . . 0—0—0—0——0

Touchdowns: *Notre Dame*—Schwartz, D. Hanley (sub for Mullins).

Points after touchdowns: *Notre Dame*—Carideo, 2.

Substitutions: *Northwestern*—Riley, Dilley, Oliphant, Moore, Gonya. *Notre Dame*—Koskey, O'Brien, D. Hanley, O'Connor, Pierce, Donoghue, Jaskwich.

Referee—H. B. Hackett, West Point. Umpire—John Schommer, Chicago. Field Judge—Fred Young, Illinois Wesleyan. Linesman—H. V. Millard, Illinois Wesleyan.

LT. GLENN WOODWARD (JUNIOR) DAVIS
(*U. S. Military Academy, '47*)

Crowning glory for Army's brightest of stars, and indicative of his exceptional all-around ability, came when Glenn Davis was voted the outstanding athlete of 1946 by the nation's sportswriters. Some even have expanded it to say that Davis is the outstanding U. S. athlete of modern times—the best since Jim Thorpe.

Three times a football All-America, an outfielder who attracted many professional baseball offers, a member of West Point's basketball team that lost only one game in 1945-46 and a brilliant sprinter on the track team, Davis' record speaks loudly for itself. Academy officials also take delight in telling of Glenn's physical-fitness record in a test which all new Cadets must take. With a perfect score of 1000 attached to the rope climbing, broad jumping, sprinting, chinning, softball throwing and obstacle course events, Davis compiled a school standard of 926½ points.

Of course, Glenn's gridiron feats have received the most publicity. A Claremont High School of California product, Davis came to West Point in 1943 with twin-brother Ralph, five minutes his senior. In three unbeaten seasons under Coach Earl (Red) Blaik, the 21-year-old Coast Comet piled up 51 touchdowns, leading the country in 1944 with 120 points.

Considered by Coach Blaik as being the fastest man he'd ever seen in a football uniform and rated by many, "the greatest halfback of modern times," Davis earned the Maxwell Memorial Trophy, Walter Camp Trophy, Heisman Award and the Los Angeles Times *Award—all emblematic of Player of the Year—during his career.*

LT. GLENN DAVIS
Army 23, Navy 7.
BALTIMORE, DECEMBER 2, 1944.

Of the many thrills I've had, I suppose the Army-Navy game of 1944 gave me my greatest. We at West Point considered that victory the best of our undefeated streak. Yes, I like that game-thrill but I can't help thinking of the time I flunked out of the Academy. I guess, whenever I think of it, that incident gives me my greatest chill.

Not many people are familiar with it, but I was dropped from West Point after my plebe year, in which I ran into scholastic trouble. Fortunately, the Academy enables you to take another exam . . . a make-up exam . . . if you desire to continue at the Point. All through the 1944 Summer I crammed and the tedious studying paid off when I passed the test and was readmitted to school. Otherwise I wouldn't be in a position today to relate the thrill I got out of the Army-Navy game in 1944.

That was a game played in Baltimore in which millions of dollars in war bonds were bought by a sellout crowd as the price of admission. Army won, 23 to 7, and there was more to it than just a victory; more to it than just a victory over Navy, too. You know what it means to a West Pointer to beat the Middies. Well, this game carried more than the regular traditional significance.

First of all, we had lost five straight games to the Tars. Rubbing salt in the deep wound was the fact that Army had scored but one

Glenn Davis, Army, three times All-America.

touchdown in those games. And, most of all, we were on the threshold of the first unbeaten Army season since 1916. Navy was the only team standing in the way of our winning the intercollegiate football championship . . . and what an obstacle!

They were great. As Coach Earl Blaik said after the game:

"I think it was a case of the country's No. 1 team beating the country's No. 2 team."

Navy was considered to have the nation's best line—Bramlett, Whitmire, Carrington, J. Martin, Chase, Gilliam and Hansen. But we had greater linemen that day in Pitzer, Arnold, Green, St. Onge, Stanowicz, Nemetz, Poole, Foldberg and Coulter.

I don't remember when we worked so hard in preparation for a game. The two-weeks practice period was spent in brisk, long drills, during which we had repeated scrimmages. Coaches Blaik, Herman Hickman, Andy Gustafson and Stu Holcomb pounded us through offensive and defensive maneuvers, leaving no stones unturned. But as the game drew closer, it became more apparent to the players that if we could handle Don Whitmire, the mastadonic tackle who made All-America at Alabama and Navy, we would win.

That job of stopping Whitmire primarily belonged to Hank Foldberg and he proceeded to play one of the greatest games of his career. It was Hank's duty to throw the blocks on the huge Whitmire and nobody envied his position; Whitmire had been tossing opposing linemen around like spitballs. Foldberg's success now is history, but more about that later.

A couple of days before the game, Captain Dick Pitzer's fallen arches began kicking up. For a while—in fact, almost until we took the field—it looked as though Pitzer's bad feet would keep him benched. Coach Blaik finally decided to go along with the badly needed end as long as he could stand on his aching feet and Pitzer gamely put out all the way.

But it wasn't only Pitzer's feet that bothered Blaik. It was Navy's feats that had our worried coach nervously pacing back and forth like an expectant loser just before we prepared to take the field. Now, Blaik wasn't the type who went in for dramatic pre-game messages. He generally issued a few last-minute instructions and then sent us out. This time, however, he walked silently up and down as we sat waiting. Finally, Coach Blaik made an unprecedented talk —for him, that is. He reached into a pocket and pulled out a telegram. It was from a buddy of his, Gen. Robert Eichelberger, one of World War II's top generals. It asked us "to win for all the soldiers scattered throughout the world," or words to that effect. That's all Blaik said.

Well, we went out and won it "for all the soldiers, etc." But more so for ourselves because, as I've said, it earned Army the national championship and helped us beat Navy after five straight defeats.

We played great team ball. Our blocking was exceptionally fine. The way our big forwards cleared out and racked up those Navy tacklers made it simple for us backs. Not that fellows like Blanchard, Kenna, Hall, Lombardo, Minor and Dobbs couldn't help themselves when the situation arose.

Our big break came when Whitmire hurt his knee on the opening kickoff. That was the start of a severe pounding from Foldberg that enabled the courageous lineman to stick it out only until late in the second period. Then he had to be helped off the field. When Don departed, he seemingly took Middie hopes for victory.

We were leading, 7 to 0, at the time on a 24-yard, second-period touchdown scored by Hall's dash through Whitmire's tackle post. When Don left the game, he carried many sensitive mementos on his body left by the shattering blocks Foldberg threw—like the one that shook Hall past the line of scrimmage for the first touchdown.

Navy fought back, though. After we had increased our lead to 9 to 0, when Stanowicz and Arnold teamed to block Hansen's third-period kick that became a safety as Hansen fell on it in the end zone, Navy started to roll.

Little Hal Hamberg took charge of the Middie attack. In the next few extremely rough moments, during which the play was furious but clean, Hamberg ran and passed to the Army one. Clyde Scott smacked over on the second try and Navy trailed, 9 to 7, after Finos' conversion.

That's the way it remained until the last quarter; until Bobby Jenkins, who had been benched by an early injury, came into the game. It was like a shot in the arm to the Navy rooters and players. Those Middie linemen started hitting us like raging madmen. Scott, Jenkins and Barron moved behind the aggressive line play into our territory. Just when it looked as though they were heading for a touchdown, the Middies got one of those tough, unpredictable breaks. Jenkins' pass sailed right into my hands.

It was Navy's last chance. Blanchard ran wild. There was no stopping him. He either picked up his interference or ran past it. From midfield, the ball was moved almost single-handedly by Doc to inside Navy's 10. There, Minor went off in motion to the left and Blanchard, on a quick-opening handoff from Lombardo, crashed over guard for the touchdown.

We got another score after that but it wasn't needed. We went 69 yards in five plays. Four of them and an offside put the ball at midfield. Blanchard took up a station as a wide flanker to the right and Minor headed the opposite way as the man-in-motion. With the defense split, Lombardo flipped me a lateral and I followed Blanchard around right end and down the sidelines for a touchdown. Minor, by the way, cut across the secondary to wipe out two defensive backs. It was easy, with that kind of blocking, to finish off a play that the boys nicknamed "The California Special." It was the first time we had used the maneuver and it helped me get my 20th touchdown and clinch the title as the country's leading scorer.

(Ed. Note—In the locker room, after the game, Davis was walking out and Army backfield coach Gustafson turned to reporters and said, "There goes one of the greatest ball carriers I have ever seen." That sentiment was echoed by Navy Coach, Cmdr. Oscar E. (Swede) Hagberg, who added: "Davis broke the game wide open for just about the best Army team that I have ever seen.")

The lineup:

ARMY (23)	pos.	NAVY (7)
Pitzer	le	Bramlett
Arnold	lt	Whitmire
Green	lg	Carrington
St. Onge	c	J. Martin
Stanowicz	rg	Chase
Nemetz	rt	Gilliam
Rafalko	re	Hansen
Kenna	qb	Duden
Hall	lh	Jenkins
Minor	rh	Barron
Blanchard	fb	Scott

Army .... 0—7—2—14——23
Navy .... 0—0—7—0——7

Touchdowns: *Army*—Hall, Blanchard, Davis. *Navy*—Scott.

Points after touchdown: *Army*—Walterhouse, 3. *Navy*—Finos.
Safety: Army.

Substitutions: *Army*—Poole, T. Hayes, Foldberg, Coulter, Webb,
R. Hays, Biles, Gerometta, Fuson, Davis, Sensanbaugher, Lom-
bardo, Dobbs, Walterhouse, Tucker. *Navy*—B. Martin, Guy,
Deramee, Shofner, Coppedge, Turner, Kiser, Baker, Hamberg,
Barskdale, Ellsworth, B. Smith, Walton, Pettit, Finos.

Referee—T. A. Timlin, Niagara. Umpire—F. S. Bergin, Princeton. Field Judge—F. R. Wallace, Washington. Linesman—
W. H. Ohrenberger, Boston College.

GLENN DOBBS, JR.

(*Tulsa, '42*)

BROOKLYN DODGERS, 1946.
LOS ANGELES DONS, 1947-   .

There are some who consider Glenn Dobbs the greatest all-around football player of the modern era. And they can't be too far wrong about the rangy, 6-foot, 4-inch 200-pounder who has been tagged a "one-man team" wherever he played.

"The Dobber," as he is called, has always been a players' player. He first entered the National spotlight at Tulsa University, where his sensational triple-threat playing gained him All-America honors in 1942. He is equally adept at punting as he is at passing and can run with the best of them.

War failed to halt Dobbs' football career. He emerged, instead, along with Bill Dudley, as the outstanding of the Service players. At Randolph Field, where he was a Lieutenant in the Air Force, and later with the Second Air Force Superbombers, he helped establish records that almost completely stole the spotlight from the colleges. His kicking has been little short of miraculous, dating back to high school days. As a schoolboy, he kicked one 80 yards and dead on the one-yard line. At Tulsa, he booted a ball 90 yards in the air, the pigskin sailing out of bounds on the two and bouncing over a head to rest finally a total of 120 yards from where it had been kicked. In the 1943 College All-Star game against the Washington Redskins he not only completed nine of 13 passes, two for touchdowns, to help the Stars win, 27 to 7, but also stood on his own goal line on one occasion and punted out of bounds on the Washington five-yard line.

Named Most Valuable Player in his first year as a professional, with Brooklyn, he led the League in 1946 in virtually every department of play. In one game, against the Yankees, he quick-kicked 78 yards.

Time alone may be the true test of greatness but if we're to judge by the past, Glenn Dobbs will undoubtedly wind up with the best.

GLENN DOBBS
Frederick, (Okla.) High School 13,
Mangum (Okla.) High 12.
MANGUM, OKLA., OCTOBER 21, 1938.

It seems strange for me to select as the greatest day of my football career a game played in high school and one in which I was only a comparatively short-time participant. I have seen great plays and players and, in my years at Tulsa, at Randolph Field, with the Second Air Force Superbombers and now in the pro game have come up against the best. But this battle of two Oklahoma high school elevens—Frederick vs. Mangum—remains as the game that will live forever in my memory.

There was, and I guess there always will be, a keen, sometimes bitter rivalry between the towns of Frederick and Mangum. No Dodger-Giant feud ever had the spirit or the fight that these two towns showed in any sort of competition, so much so that the feeling was more intense with the towns than with the competing teams themselves.

Our team at Frederick came up to the traditional game with Mangum owning an undefeated record. Our coach, John Gregg, a former Hardin-Simmons athlete, is the finest coach I have ever played under, and I say that in all respect to the coaches I've had. I really mean it. He showed us, he didn't just tell us. He was the first who ever impressed on me that, when you kick, the most im-

Glenn Dobbs, one of pro football's greatest passers.

portant thing is to drop the ball right. He showed me that in passing it isn't just a hit-or-miss proposition. "Hit the receiver with it," he said, "and then it's his problem, not yours."

Mangum had a much larger team than ours, and we were not figured to win, despite our good record. We had only about 14 or 15 men who did all the playing and I was only a kid who could punt or pass. There are factors in football, however, that make good little men great and that's what happened that cool Oklahoma evening.

Early in the first quarter, with each team merely feeling the other out, I punted out on their eight-yard line. It was one of those punts that you get off occasionally when luck is with you and it was a bad break for Mangum. The whistle blew when the ball went out and as I was going down the field, a Mangum player threw a block at me. I pushed him down to the ground and when he got up, he slapped me on the shoulder and smilingly said:

"Nice kick."

The referee rushed up and put us both out of the game for slugging.

Controversy still rages over that play and even got to the stage where some people close to the situation virtually called it a "frame-up." It certainly isn't within my power to call it that but the facts pointed to it and left a bitterness between the two towns that took years to erase. The "break" against us, which took from our team the only passer and kicker, turned an outmanned, outpowered eleven into an emotionally inspired aggregation that bordered on greatness.

I will never forget the period before I left the field. The argument was long and fierce but futile. When I departed, our team, with all the boys crying, declared they would win this one. It wasn't in the books for us to win but they had reached the emotional pitch that is rare among athletes.

We had no tailback now, so our blocking back moved to that position. We had no punter, but our left guard said he'd punt. Both his hands were injured so badly that he had to wear a stiff leather guard on each hand. These were taped so that his hands were practically in casts. That was Bobby Raley, the kid who lived next door to me, and who later went on to become a good halfback at Centenary.

Our boys were so mad, determined and courageous that they went out and played the finest ball game I have ever seen, bar none —and what made it more thrilling was that they had told me that they were playing this one for me. Raley put on one of the finest punting exhibitions I have ever seen, and the blocking back, Jack Weathers, ran the team as if he'd done it all his life.

Both our touchdowns were scored on passes from Weathers. In the first period he hit Overton with a short one for a touchdown, and he contacted with another pass to Blanton in the third period for the other. Raley place-kicked the extra point after the second touchdown and that proved to be our margin of victory.

Yes, our ball club was really hot that night—a heat stirred by anger and determination. Our line charged as if they were all 200-pounders instead of averaging only about 147. Our backs ran, blocked and tackled like madmen. For three periods, we held Mangum scoreless, breaking up every one of their desperate drives—that broke the Mangum spirit, too. It was not until the fourth quarter that they were able to score, one touchdown on a ground play, and the other on a long pass from Bates to Tillman. Both their extra point kicks, aimed by a team whose "backs" were virtually broken by a power they couldn't cope with or understand, missed—and that told the story.

I had absolutely nothing to do with the result of that game—the greatest day or victory in my book. The game was only three minutes old, and the score 0 to 0 when I left. However, to me, that will always be the finest thing I ever got out of playing football. We weren't supposed to win even at full strength, yet those boys won that game in good shape, and we went through the rest of the season undefeated and untied.

The years have made me lose contact with a lot of those boys. None of them had the opportunity to go on to college stardom but that one night, under the Oklahoma stars, eleven "All-Americas" played the most brilliant game of football I have ever seen.

The lineup:
FREDERICK
(13)   pos.   MANGUM (12)
Langham   .....le....... Hogue
Gover   ....lt....... McCall

Raley ....lg....... Roach
Tucker ....c....... Greasby
Pritchard ....rg....... McGregor
Wade ....rt....... Cummings
Smith ....re....... Mallard
Dobbs ....qb....... Bates
Weathers ......lh....... Boyle
Overton ....rh....... Smith
Heady ....fb....... Tillman
Frederick ....6—0—7—0——13
Mangum ....0—0—0—12——12

Touchdowns: *Frederick*—Overton (pass from Weathers) *Blanton*—(pass from Weathers); *Mangum*—Hollis, Bates.
Points after touchdown: *Frederick*—Raley (placement).

WILLIAM M. (BILL) DUDLEY
(*Virginia, '42*)
PITTSBURGH STEELERS, 1942; 1945-1946.
DETROIT LIONS, 1947-   .

"Not exceptionally fast, Dudley depends on hard running, unshakable confidence and a terrific desire to play football to make himself a top notch pro ball player."

That's the way the Pittsburgh Steelers' 1946 brochure described the Bluefield Bullet, who as a 19-year-old senior at Virginia had led the 1941 collegiate scoring parade with 134 points. In two full seasons with Pittsburgh, Dudley wrote his name on the historic pages of the National Football League.

As a freshman, in 1942, Bullet Bill led the league in ground gaining and was honored with a place on the All-Star team. Returning in 1945, after three years of B-29 piloting, he played but three games for the Steelers and yet became their leading scorer.

In 1946, Dudley reached his heights. He came close to being acclaimed the best all-around player in the country. He not only led the league in ground gaining but was also the team's top passer, finished fifth in scoring with five touchdowns, 12 extra points and two field goals, and was honored with the League's Most Valuable Player award. Defensively, particularly against forward passes, there were few, if any, who could surpass him.

On the verge of quitting the pro game to take a coaching job, Dudley was sold to the Detroit Lions and despite the fact that the Lions were woefully weak, Dudley always made his presence felt. The 5 foot, 10 inch West Virginian, who weighs a puny 170 compared to the massive bone-crushers who face him, holds his own in any company where football is played.

Dudley must have been good to make All-America in 1941 and the little guy from a "little" school did just that. He is, without doubt, one of the greatest triple-threat backs ever developed in the South.

BILL DUDLEY
Virginia 28, North Carolina 7.
CHAPEL HILL, N. C., NOVEMBER 20, 1941.

In 1941, Virginia won nine games and lost only to Yale, 21 to 19. They all mattered to us Cavaliers, but none like the 28-7 conquest of North Carolina. When I tell you that North Carolina had beaten us eight years in a row and thirteen out of fourteen, and we had never scored a victory at Chapel Hill since the traditional series started in 1892, then you'll realize why I favor this game above all others.

The newspapers hailed it as "Bill Dudley Day" because I chalked up 22 points and passed to the other touchdown. But you know that one man isn't a whole team—especially a football team. Our fellows formed one of the most inspired bunch of players ever to appear on a gridiron and they played their hearts out for Coach Frank Murray.

When we walked off the Kenan Stadium Field that afternoon we were the most tired but happy kids in America. I was particularly overjoyed in having the best day of my career fall on my last collegiate football game and in one that was so important to Virginia. There's an amazing school spirit here at Charlottesville, Virginia, and even the incoming freshmen learn quickly of the historic days when Virginia was a leading power on the football scene. We were proud to have brought back a few memories of the old times.

The writers raved about my passing to Bill Preston for a 21-yard touchdown in the first period; running 67 yards for another in

*Bill Dudley, ace half back who played at Virginia before entering
pro football.*

the same period; running 79 yards for a third touchdown in the third quarter, and scoring the last one on a three-yard plunge in the final period. Sure, all that's fine stuff for the naked eye. But I knew what was behind it, fellows like our ends, rangy Preston, who caught 22 passes that year for 377 yards and made the National honor roll, and little Billy Hill . . . Eddie Bryant . . . Bill Suhling . . . Jack Sauerback . . . Herb Munhall . . . Howie Goodwin . . . Johnny Neff . . . et al. The whole Virginia team blocked like fiends that afternoon. And the downfield blocking of Hill was something to see.

That 67-yard run of mine, for instance, which produced the second touchdown, was credited as being a bit of foxy running. Bryant, however, took out the Carolina end with as pretty a block as you'll catch anywhere. If he hadn't been there, I'd have been dropped at the line of scrimmage. That's the way it was all afternoon.

It's unfortunate that the records of a game don't show what every man on the team did. Without the help of my teammates I could never have carried the ball 215 yards on 17 attempts for a 12.6 average, completed six of 11 passes for 117 yards, averaged 39.3 yards from the line of scrimmage with eight punts and scored the points I did.

The game enabled me to capture the scoring title in the College race with 134 points and 18 touchdowns but the greatest feeling of pleasure I ever had came at the end when the finest bunch of men a guy ever played with carried me off the field on their shoulders.

The lineup:

VIRGINIA (28)	pos.	NORTH CAROLINA (7)
Hill	le	Hodges
Steckmesser	lt	Sieck
Fuller	lg	Nowell
Suhling	c	Benton
Sauerbeck	rg	Faircloth
Schlegel	rt	White
Preston	re	Richardson
Neff	qb	Austin
Dudley	lh	Dunkle
Goodwin	rh	Barksdale
Munhall	fb	O'Hare
Virginia	14—0—7—7——28	
North Carolina	7—0—0—0——7	

Touchdowns: *Virginia*—Dudley, 3, Preston. *North Carolina*—Barksdale.

Points after touchdown: *Virginia*—Dudley, 4. *North Carolina*—Dunkle.

Substitutions: *Virginia*—Rhett, Abbott, White, Schlesinger, Oahmig, Mirman, Parlow, Bear, C. Cooper, Lakin, Seiler, Gillette, Craig, West, Crenshaw, Kreick, Nikalson, Bryant, Marshall.

North Carolina—Elliott, Turner, Crone, Stallings, Michaels, Lewis, Graham, Wolf, Cheek, Wood, Pecora, Herlich, Gugert, Sigler, Jordan, Baker, Cox.

ALBERT GLEN (TURK) EDWARDS
(*Washington State, '32*)
BOSTON-WASHINGTON REDSKINS, 1932- .

Tackles don't come much better than Turk Edwards.

The Northwest giant, who earned All-America honors in four brilliant years at Washington State moved into the professional game and became one of its all-time greats.

Some men are known for their tackling, but what really made Turk an unusual power was his ability to tackle coupled with an almost uncanny knack of blocking kicks and rushing passers.

Edwards became a member of the Boston eleven in 1932. He was one of the original players of a unit formed by George Marshall in his first year as a National League franchise owner. He went with Marshall when the team moved to Washington in 1937 and the fact that he is still with them is a tribute not only to his talents as a player and a coach but also to his astute character.

Turk became the seventh head coach in Redskin history, following on the heels of Lud Wray, Lone Star Dietz, Eddie Casey, Ray Flaherty, Dutch Bergman and Dud DeGroot. He assumed the role in 1946 and immediately served notice on the League that his teams were to be reckoned with. He piloted the Redskins into second place in his first year, not bad for a fellow with the tremendous task of rebuilding a team that had slowly lost many of its stars to Time and war.

Reluctantly, Edwards will admit that he also played a little basketball, but the records show he was an outstanding court man on the Pacific Coast.

TURK EDWARDS
Washington State 14, Oregon State 7.
PORTLAND, ORE., NOVEMBER 1, 1930.

There were three minutes left to play and the score was 7 to 7 in this important battle between Washington State and Oregon State.

Oregon State's Buerke faded back to pass. They weren't satisfied with an almost certain tie—they wanted to win our traditional battle. They were the underdog in this game. A defeat might keep us from winning the Pacific Coast Conference championship, and the Rose Bowl which a Washington State eleven hadn't visited since 1916.

And as Buerke went back for the pass, the entire future of the season hinged on what happened. A Buerke-to-Root forward had enabled Oregon State to tie the score early in the fourth period. Buerke was one of the outstanding passers on the Pacific Coast. In one game that season, he had passed 54 yards to Root on the three for a touchdown. This pass had to be stopped—but how.

Ahlskog, at right tackle, and I, at left tackle, had the same thing in mind. As Buerke raised his arm, we both charged across the scrimmage line. The ball left Buerke's hand just as Ahlskog's hand came up to meet it. The ball hit my co-tackle's hand. I saw all that in time to change my course. I scooped up the deflected ball before it hit the ground and like a frightened rabbit raced 30 yards for the touchdown that gave our Cougars the ball game.

It isn't often that a tackle scores a touchdown—and what a tremendous thrill that was, especially to a lumbering man like myself, 6 feet, 2½ inches in height and weighing a mere 235 at the time. It was fortunate that Ahlskog got to the ball to deflect it before I did. Had we both hit there at the same time, the ball game would have undoubtedly ended in a tie. Those are the breaks.

The Oregon State-Washington State rivalry dates back to 1903 and has been one of the most fiercely fought series anywhere in football. The highest score ever made in one of our games reached the big total of 29 points. In my career at Washington State we beat them four successive years on scores of 9 to 7, 9 to 0, 14 to 7, and 7 to 6, which will give you a fair idea of how close our games have been.

There was an amazing spirit at Washington State in 1930. Under Orin Hollingbery, we had been knocking at the door of the Pacific Coast championship but could never quite make it. The last time the Cougars had turned the trick was actually in 1916, although they wound up in a three-way tie in 1917.

With 32,600 fans in the stands, the second largest crowd ever to see a game in Portland, we had to hurdle this stubborn Beaver eleven. Paul Schissler had molded an underrated team at Oregon State and this particular day they were also an inspired team. We entered the game full of confidence, however. On succeeding Saturdays we had defeated the perennial powerhouses of the Coast League —U.S.C. and California. Newspapers pounded us on our respective backs daily, hailing us as sure-fire National championship timber.

Nothing happened to temper our optimism at the game's start. In fact, when halfback Ellingsen got off on a long touchdown run around Oregon State's end and Maskell booted the point for a 7-0 lead, we had visions of a runaway. These visions vanished quickly.

The Beavers played our powerful forward wall to a scoreless standstill in the second and third periods. In place of confidence, there appeared the frightful spectre of an upset when the Beavers, twice-stopped on our five-yard line, tied the score on Buerke's pass to Root. The breaks seemed to go against us, too, when an offside penalty against our over-anxious line gave them the extra point automatically instead of kicking—a kick we hoped to block. In those days, a penalty against the defense on the conversion attempt gave the offense an automatic extra point.

It looked bad for the Cougars as the minutes ticked away and then, of course, came that one deciding pass play that led to my score, and gave me my greatest day in football.

Washington State finished the season unbeaten and untied and though we went on to be soundly beaten by Alabama, 24 to 0, in the Rose Bowl, we still gained second place in the poll for the National championship. One of my teammates on the Cougar eleven was Mel Hein, the same Mel Hein who for 14 years was one of the great centers of the National Football League with the New York Giants. I've had many thrills since, too, one of them being my appointment as head coach of the Washington Redskins, and another playing with fellows like Sammy Baugh and Cliff Battles. I doubt, however, if I'll ever get the kick out of a day as I did when I carried my big hulk those 30 yards to a touchdown for Washington State.

The lineup:

WASHINGTON STATE (14)	pos.	OREGON STATE (7)
Maskell	le	McKalip
Edwards	lt	Kent
Parodi	lg	Cox
Hein	c	Hammer
G. Hurley	rg	Thompson
Ahlskog	rt	Miller
J. Hurley	re	McGilvray
Tonkin	qb	Buerke
Ellingsen	lh	Sherwood
Larnhart	rh	Moe
Schwartz	fb	Little

Washington State ..... 7—0—0—7——14
Oregon State ..... 0—0—0—7——7

Touchdowns: *Washington State*—Ellingsen, Edwards. *Oregon State*—Root (sub for McGilvray).

Points after touchdowns: *Washington State*—Maskell, 2. *Oregon State*—Washington State offside.

Referee—George Varnell. Umpire—Bruce Kirkpatrick. Linesman—Bobby Monis. Field Judge—Sky Huntington.

BEATTIE FEATHERS
(Tennessee, '34)
CHICAGO BEARS, 1934-1937.
BROOKLYN DODGERS, 1938-1939.
GREEN BAY PACKERS, 1940.
APPALACHIAN STATE TEACHERS, 1942.
NORTH CAROLINA STATE, 1944-   .

Beattie Feathers was just a natural athlete. As a Tennessee undergraduate, he gained eight letters in football, track and basketball. Then, when he moved into the pro field, he gained prominence as a baseball as well as a football player.

Before going to the Chicago Bears in 1934, Feathers left his mark in intercollegiate circles. During the 1933 season, to climax a great collegiate career, he gained 1052 yards in 10 games for a 9.0 average. He was unanimously selected for All-America honors, was voted the Most Valuable Player in the star-studded Southeastern Conference. Chosen by the fans to appear in the first-annual Chicago All-Star game against the Bears in 1934, he was a big factor in holding the Professional champions to a scoreless deadlock.

Rated one of the greatest runners ever produced in the South, Feathers was a sensation with the Bears in 1934 and his record of 1004 yards gained in 101 attempts has yet to be erased from the books. He was chosen All-League halfback in 1934 and as long as he remained in pro football was always a top player.

As a coach, he has had only fair success but is regarded as a fine developer of talent and since his arrival at North Carolina State in 1944 has moved them from a mediocre spot to the tag of "always dangerous." And that's the way he played, too—whenever he got the ball, Beattie Feathers was always dangerous.

BEATTIE FEATHERS
North Carolina State 13, Duke 6.
RALEIGH, N. C., SEPTEMBER 28, 1946.

When a team you're coaching is a decided underdog and can defeat a Wallace Wade-coached Duke eleven, then you've just had a great day. I've had thrills and days as a player but none compares with that of pointing and priming a team for a game that it goes out to win against the longest of odds.

The last time North Carolina State had beaten Duke was away back in 1932. Since then they had walloped the Wolfpack in twelve successive meetings, including a drubbing of 75 to 0, in 1943, the year before I came to Raleigh. I, too, had a score to settle with the Blue Devils. They had beaten our Tennessee team of 1933, 10 to 2, and that was my last year as a college player.

As we came up for the game, there was little hope for us. It was the opening game of the season and looked on as a "breather" for the Blue Devils. You just can't send a team out on the field with orders to win. You tell them to play hard and to fight to the last gun but you can't demand, particularly when you're supposedly outmanned in every department.

Wade had just returned to Duke after a long war service. He had fine personnel at his disposal in fellows like Ernie (Bear) Knotts, George Clark and Bob Gantt. They were rated so highly that this ball game was considered just the first stop on their road to a certain Southern Conference title and a Bowl bid.

Beattie Feathers, All-America at Tennessee before joining Chicago's Bears and present coach at N. Carolina State.

Right at the start, we got a tough break that would have broken the spirit of most teams. But this outfit, destined to become one of the finest in Wolfpack history, took the misfortune in stride and battled all the more furiously.

We were backed up against our goal line when Knotts pounced on one of our fumbles that had been slithering around in the mud caused by a heavy rain. It was first down and touchdown to go from our seven for Duke. And, on the first play, Clark raced around end for a lead that remained at 6 to 0 when Gantt missed the extra point try.

That lead looked big as the game progressed. Hampered by the poor playing conditions, we fought the Blue Devils to a standstill in the second period and left the field at halftime still trailing, 6 to 0, and cursing our luck and the bad weather. Little were we to know at the time that the same bad weather was going to help us tie the score at the start of the second half.

Duke seemed to be moving along on a threatening drive when a lateral eluded Buddy Mulligan on the slippery field. Halfback Oscar Bozeman recovered for us on our 44. Then, halfback Charley Richkus, who was the individual hero of this game, sparked a march that brought us to the Duke 12. He completely disregarded the elements and flipped a pass into the end zone where Bozeman made a sensational touchdown catch. The score remained knotted as Jim Byler failed to convert.

Our tough line, which had slowed down the highly-heralded Duke attack, continued to outplay the Blue Devils. But at the same time, we couldn't make any progress against Wade's defense. The deadlock looked like a permanent one—that is, until we threw caution to the wind and the rain in the closing minutes.

Our All-Southern halfback, Howard Turner, and Richkus, took hold of a wet ball and amazed the crowd with a passing attack that will never be forgotten by those who saw it. From our 25, we marched to the Duke four. There, with only 10 seconds left, Richkus smashed over the goal line. Byler's extra point only served to add the finishing touch to a game well won and at the time considered one of the biggest upsets in Southern football history.

Duke never recovered from that opening game blow and went on a mediocre season. On the other hand, we finished with an eight won, two lost, record, one of the finest in Wolfpack annals.

The smashing of the 12-year Duke reign was a thrill enjoyed by all connected with Wolfpack football. The long runs and touchdowns made as a player can't compare with the real pleasure of seeing my own team achieve greatness, even for a day.

The lineup:
N. C. STATE

(13)	pos.	DUKE (6)
Phillips	le	Mote
Ramsey	lt	Hardison
Watts	lg	Knotts
Saunders	c	Wall
Wagoner	rg	Milner
Dressler	rt	Derogatis
Gibson	re	Duncan
Bowlby	qb	Gantt
Turner	lh	Mulligan
Bozeman	rh	Clark
Palmer	fb	Long

N. C. State .... 0—0—6—7——13
Duke .... 6—0—0—0——6

Touchdowns: *Duke*—Clark. *N. C. State*—Bozeman, Richkus.
Points after touchdown: *N. C. State*—Byler

Substitutions: *North Carolina State*—Courts, Blomquist, Dressler, Miller, F. Wagoner, Rees, Byler, J. Wagoner, Burnett, R. Gibson, Fletcher, Richkus, Goodman, Sheets, Smith, J. Gibson, Allen, Durant. *Duke*—Cittadino, Karmazin, Smith, Mullins, Allen, Oenbring, Chambers, W. Davis, Wolfe, C. Davis, Folger, Hartley, Montgomery, Inman, Luper, Williams, Strouss.

Referee—J. D. Rogers, Jr., Washington & Lee. Umpire—R. A. Collier, Wake Forest. Field Judge—Joby Hawn, Lenoir-Rhyne. Head Linesman—George Compton, Randolph Macon.

GEORGE (THE GIPPER) GIPP
(*Notre Dame, 1917-1920*)

George Gipp was Notre Dame's greatest football player.

The opinion belongs to the late Knute Rockne and is shared by thousands of fans and experts who saw this amazing "natural" in action. Gipp could do everything in athletics and the world lost one of sportsdom's most extraordinary products when the Gipper succumbed to pneumonia in 1920, the year he was unanimously acclaimed All-America fullback.

The exploits of the Gipper on and off the football field are legend in the history of the gridiron game. There is the story of his performance in a game against Western Normal. He was a freshman then and Notre Dame had no punter that year. A punt was needed and none of the boys would leave the game to let a punter come in. It was Gipp who saved the situation.

"I can't punt," he said simply, "but I can dropkick pretty well. It'll be as good as a punt."

They lined up for the play and Gipp dropkicked, as he put it "as far as I could." The ball not only traveled 62 yards in the air over the goal line but also went over the goal posts—one of the longest dropkicks for a field goal on record.

He was as unpredictable as he was brilliant. In the 1920 game against Army, Notre Dame wasn't doing so well when the half ended. Rockne tore into the players in the dressing room, looked up suddenly and saw Gipp calmly smoking a cigarette seemingly oblivious to the fiery pep talk.

"And you, Mr. Gipp," Rockne burst forth scornfully, "I suppose you don't care whether we win or not."

"That's where you're wrong, Rock," quietly replied the Gipper. "I've got 500 bucks on this game."

With Gipp giving one of the most remarkable one-man performances ever seen, Notre Dame swept through Army in the second half to win, 27 to 17.

That was the Gipper, whose name will live forever in American football annals.

GEORGE GIPP
Notre Dame 13, Indiana 10.
BLOOMINGTON, IND., NOVEMBER 30, 1920.

**(as told by Walter Kennedy, Publicity Director at Notre Dame
in the Rockne Era)**

Whenever Notre Dame men meet, the talk invariably turns to football and particularly about those Irish gridiron heroes over the years who have made pigskin history with their exploits. Every Notre Dame man has his particular favorite for whom he'll talk and argue for hours in an attempt to convince his listeners that he was the "greatest of them all." But deep down in his heart, every Notre Dame man has a special niche in his memory for one player who was probably the greatest of all of the great Irish football players.

That was George Gipp, the legendary figure who came out of Laurium, Michigan, to help Knute Rockne place Notre Dame at the pinnacle of football glory in the years of and after World War I. Most people know the story of Gipp. How Rockne saw him kicking a football on the Notre Dame campus in street shoes, booting the ball far and wide. How Rock asked him to come out for the team, and how Gipp brashly said, "I like baseball, that's my game. I haven't any interest in football." They know, too, that Gipp finally did go out for the frosh team that same year. In his very first game, against Western Normal, he drop-kicked a 62-yard field goal, breaking a tie in the last three minutes of the game, thus starting his fabulous career. That kick still stands in the record books, although over 30 years have elapsed.

But most people do not know other things about George Gipp. He was one of the best pool and billiard players in the country, and traveling "sharks" of those days, who used to hit South Bend in search of suckers, came to know him as a player surpassing even their great ability. Gipp was a fine card player, too, and possessed that gambler's instinct that gave him an insight into the worth of his hand, and those of his opponents, long before the others were aware of those matters.

It has often been said that Gipp was not a good student. This is far from the truth. Gipp was an excellent scholar, but he didn't have the time or patience to study. It was characteristic of his academic work, as it was with his football and baseball playing, that all he needed was a "shower and shave" to be ready for whatever confronted him. He had the rare ability to diagnose, whether it be an opponent's football play, a pitcher's next pitch or a professor's examination question. In his studies, he just "got by." In athletics, he was the best.

It is difficult to pick out Gipp's best game, because he starred in practically every one he participated in during his career. His feats against Army are widely known, especially the 1920 game, when Gipp passed, kicked and ran the Irish to a 27-17 win, after the Kaydets led 7 to 0.

But most old-timers say that his performance against Indiana in 1920 was his greatest. Legend has it that Gipp broke his collar bone the night before the game, but that Rockne never knew it. In the first period, Gipp was hurt and it was discovered then, officially at least, that he had a dislocated shoulder and broken collar bone. He was taken off the field and sat huddled next to Rock on the bench. The game was viciously played, and going into the last quarter Indiana led by a 10-0 score.

Gipp pleaded with Rock to be allowed back in the game, but Rockne paid no attention to him. Finally, the Irish got rolling and, sparked by Johnny Mohardt's 25-yard run and Norm Barry's inspired play as Gipp's sub, finally reached the one-foot marker. At this point, Rock turned to Gipp, peeled off his blanket and told him to go in and get that ball across. It was a spot where a touch of the Gipp power was needed. He took the ball, lugged it into pay dirt and kicked the goal, but Indiana still led, 10 to 7.

Gipp kicked off. Indiana could not gain and Notre Dame took over. Gipp, suffering excruciating pain and unable to pass normally, used a side-arm movement instead of the overhand throw. His passing and running soon brought the ball down to the 15-yard line. This was a place for a Gipp dropkick to tie the score, because he was almost automatic from that distance. But Gipp wasn't playing for a tie. He knew Indiana expected Notre Dame to play cozy and figured it would watch out for his kick. So he whispered to Joe Brandy in the huddle, they lined up and instead of a kick, Gipp whipped a pass to Eddie Anderson, good for a first down on the one-yard line. Once again Indiana set themselves for a Gipp crack at the line. But again Gipp fooled them. While they watched his every move and piled him up on the line of scrimmage, Brandy ploughed over for the second touchdown of the period to give Notre Dame the game, 13 to 10. It was the closest call they had during their undefeated 1920 season and newspaper articles of the time say it was one of the most brutal games of football ever played.

Less than a month later, Gipp was dead. The following week after his great playing against Indiana, the Gipper was stricken with pneumonia and a strep throat and died in South Bend on December 14. The day he died Rockne informed Gipp that he had been selected by Walter Camp on his All-America team, the first Notre Dame player ever so honored.

The lineup:
NOTRE DAME

(13)	pos.	INDIANA (10)
Kiley	le	Bell
Coughlin	lt	Risley
H. Anderson	lg	McGaw
Larson	c	Pierce
Smith	rg	Mumby
Shaw	rt	Leonard
E. Anderson	re	Haney
Brandy	qb	Mathys
Gipp	lh	Thomas
Mohardt	rh	Minton
Wynne	fb	Kyle

Notre Dame ....0—0—0—13——13
Indiana ....0—3—7—0——10
Touchdowns: *Notre Dame*—Gipp, Brandy. *Indiana*—Haney.
Points after touchdowns: *Notre Dame*—Gipp (dropkick). *Indiana*—Risley (placement).
Field Goal: *Indiana*—Risley (placement).

GEORGE S. HALAS
(Illinois, '18)
CHICAGO BEARS, 1921-   .

Synonymous with the name Chicago Bears, is the T-Formation and George Halas, head-man and head-coach of the team that over a period of years has been called the greatest football machine of all time.

After four years of football and football lore under the famous Bob Zuppke at Illinois, Halas organized a team known as Staley's of Decatur, Ill., in 1920; moved it to Chicago in 1921; changed its name to the Bears—and has been clawing them apart ever since. While he never claimed inventing the T-Formation, there are few who will dispute the fact that, under his coaching and the expert quarterbacking of such stars as Boyd Brumbaugh, Bernie Masterson and Sid Luckman, the Bears have perfected the game's most popular attack.

Halas was a better than average football flanker, captained the Illinois basketball team, and even played a piece of baseball for the New York Yankees—but his record with the Bears has far surpassed his accomplishments as an athlete. The record:

National League Champions—1921, 1932. (No playoffs)

National League Champions—Playoff system—1933-1940-1941-1943-1946.

Western Division Champions—1933-1934-1937-1940-1941-1942-1943-1944-1946.

And not to be outdone, however, by his galaxy of stars who have paraded to glory in the Bear uniform, Halas still holds the league record for the "longest run with a fumble"—98 yards to a touchdown for the Bears against the Canton Bulldogs in 1922.

GEORGE HALAS
Chicago Bears 73, Washington Redskins 0.
NATIONAL LEAGUE CHAMPIONSHIP, WASHINGTON, D. C.,
DECEMBER 8, 1940.

The 1940 National League championship victory of the Chicago
Bears over the Washington Redskins at Griffith Stadium will always
stand out in my memory as the most sensational football contest I
have ever witnessed or was fortunate enough to have a part in.

It is one of those days that happens once in a lifetime in a football league as tough as ours. The Bears executed plays almost to
perfection that day. They blocked and tackled with precision force—
the score talks for the offense. And the Redskins played good football in spite of the score.

A reporter once asked Charley Malone, a Washington end in
that memorable game, what the score might have been had he not
dropped a pass in the end zone early in that game.

"The score would have been 73 to 7," replied Malone.

It seemed as though the Bears couldn't do anything wrong.

There's a story behind that victory and while I don't know if it
affected the final score it certainly was evidence that the Bears were
determined to beat the Redskins. On November 17th, in Washington, the Redskins had beaten us, 7 to 3, in a rough struggle. On what
was virtually the last play of the game, Sid Luckman fired a pass to
George McAfee in the end zone. That could have been the winning

George Halas, the Big Bear and his clawing cubs.

touchdown. The Redskins, however, swarmed over McAfee, and that pass was never caught.

We thought it was interference but the referee thought otherwise and that's the way it ended. The newspapers, however, picked up the dispute and slowly fanned it into a raging inferno. They quoted George Marshall, Redskin owner, as saying:

"The Bears are just a first-half team."

It didn't take much to keep that fire burning among the Bears. As game time approached, they were a grim, determined group of athletes with one thought in mind—to win. The Redskins were cocky, confident of duplicating their earlier triumph. They didn't change their defense for us. Luckman was quick to see that.

The game was only 56 seconds old when the parade began. Luckman faked to the right and handed the ball to Bullet Bill Osmanski on a quick-opening play to his left. Osmanski shot through a hole as the Bear line cleared his path. George Wilson took out two remaining secondaries with one ferocious block and Osmanski raced 68 yards unmolested for the first score.

Washington had a fleeting chance to alter the course of the pendulum. This was when Malone dropped the aforementioned pass from Sammy Baugh on the goal line in the early moments of the game. Washington had one other good scoring opportunity, right after Osmanski's opening run when it marched to the Bears' 22, but Bob Masterson missed a field goal. Then the flood gates opened wide.

The avalanche produced three touchdowns in the first period, one in the second, four in the third and three in the last. What made the Bears' performance all the more spectacular was the fact that the final score was a combination of the 7-3 score we had lost by. We made orthodox touchdowns and we made others by interceptions. Nothing like it had ever been seen on any gridiron in a game between two top teams—and Washington was far from a weak team. The climactic touch was produced after our eleventh touchdown when the referee came over to me.

"George," said the referee, "the ball we're using now is the only one we have left. Would you mind not kicking for the extra point? Please throw a forward pass instead."

And so my Bears, like the nice little gentlemen they are, threw a pass.

It's difficult to conceive a 73-0 score but it happened. Eighty yards and 17 plays after Osmanski's touchdown, Chicago scored again, Luckman sneaking over from six inches out. Then Joe Maniaci roared off on a 42-yard scoring gallop and it was 21 to 0, thanks to the added points from the toes of Automatic Jack Manders, Bob Snyder and Phil Martinovich.

The Washington faithful among the 36,034 fans were stunned. Still, the worst was yet to come.

Early in the second quarter, the Bears fumbled on the 'Skins 16, giving the home team a chance to march to the Chicago 18. Taking the ball on downs, the Bears bounced back to the Washington 24 from where Martinovich missed a field goal try.

Ray Nolting then set up the fourth touchdown with the first of eight Bear interceptions. Ground plays picked up 26 yards and Luckman passed the remaining 30 to Ken Kavanaugh standing in the end zone. Snyder converted and it was 28 to 0.

Fifty-four seconds after the second half opening whistle the Bears counted touchdown No. 5. Baugh's lateral was intercepted by end Hampton Pool on the Redskin 16 and carried across. That was enough to make Washington desperate and disgusted, as it proved by tossing a fourth down pass from its 33 that was batted down.

The Bears accepted the charity. Nolting warmed up with a 10-yard romp. Then, he cracked over center, feinted Baugh out of his path and registered the sixth. No sooner did Washington take the ball than the Bears rolled up another touchdown. Roy Zimmerman's pass was intercepted by George McAfee, who raced 35 yards through a broken field for the tally.

Shortly thereafter, another Zimmerman pass led to touchdown No. 8. This time it was center Bulldog Turner who intercepted on the Washington 30 and rumbled over, behind a neat block by Pool, making it 54 to 0. By now, nobody cared who was trying to boot the extra point.

The Western division champs did it the hard way on the ninth touchdown, marching 74 yards as the fourth quarter started. Harry Clark was the point-getter with a 42-yard sprint on the end of a double-reverse.

Washington found another way to gift the Bears, who hardly needed it, with their next touchdown opportunity. Frank Filchock fumbled on his two and 300-pound Jack Torrance, the world's shot-put record-holder, fell on the ball. Gary Famiglietti banged it over on a quick opener. That brought the Bears down to their 11th and last touchdown. It came on Clark's one-yard burst through the middle, climaxing a 52-yard drive. Snyder passed to Maniaci for the conversion to conserve the ball supply, but the throw fell incomplete. The final whistle blew mercifully a few moments later.

It must have been a humiliating defeat for George Marshall, a good friend—off the football field—and for the Redskin players. It was the worst beating ever administered in pro history and, on the other hand, the greatest victory ever scored. The Bears rolled up 372 yards rushing to Washington's three. But, and here's something Bob Ripley wouldn't believe, the Redskins earned 18 first downs to the Bears' 17.

That was the day of days for football.

The lineup:
BEARS (73)   pos.   REDSKINS (0)
Nowaskey ......le........ Masterson
Stydahar ....lg........ Wilkin

Fortmann ....lt....... Farman
Turner ....c....... Titchenal
Musso ....rg....... Silvinski
Artoe ....rt....... Barber
Wilson ....re....... Malone
Luckman .....qb....... Krause
Nolting ....lh....... Baugh
McAfee ....rh....... Justice
Osmanski ......fb....... Johnston
Bears ....21—7—26—19——73
Redskins ....0—0—0—0——0

Touchdowns: Chicago—Clark, 2, Osmanski, Luckman, Maniaci, Kavanaugh, Nolting, Pool, McAfee, Turner, Famiglietti.

Points after touchdowns: Chicago—Manders, Snyder, 2, Martinovich, Plasman, Stydahar, Maniaci.

Substitutions: Bears—Siegal, Manske, Plasman, Pool, Kavanaugh, Mihal, Kolman, Torrance, Martinovich, Forte, Baisi, Bausch, Chesney, Famiglietti, Clark, Manders, Maniaci, Snyder, Sherman, Masterson, Swisher, McLean. Redskins—McChesney, Sanford, Millner, Fisher, Russell, Stralka, Shugart, Andrako, Parks, Pinckert, Morgan, Seymour, Zimmerman, Filchock, Moore, Todd, Hare, Hoffman, Farkas, Meade.

Referee—W. E. Friesell, Princeton. Umpire—Harry Robb, Penn State. Field Judge—Fred Young, Illinois Wesleyan. Head Linesman—Irving Kupcinet, North Dakota.

MELVIN JOHN (MEL) HEIN
(*Washington State, '31*)
NEW YORK GIANTS, 1932-1945.
UNION COLLEGE, 1946.
LOS ANGELES DONS, 1947-   .

Impeding the United States mails brought Mel Hein to the New York Giants. The Washington State lineman, who is considered by football authorities as the greatest center of all time, had already signed a contract to play with Providence. The contract was in the mails but for once the Post Office slogan of getting the mail through, failed. It failed because of Ray Flaherty, then a Giant end, and two cooperative postmasters who helped intercept the document before it reached Providence. It saved Hein for the Giants.

Few football players ever gained the personal popularity that Mel did in New York—and to celebrate his 10th anniversary with the Giants the fans made it "Mel Hein Day" in December, 1940.

A guard at the start, Hein gained All-League honors in 1933 and 1934. Then he started a string of All-League center selections that ran unbroken through the 1940 campaign. His coach, Steve Owen, has this to say about Hein:

"I can count on the fingers of one hand the mistakes he made offensively and defensively. Mel never missed a championship game. He needed time out on only two occasions in 15 years of bruising pro football. A great team player and a wonderful inspiration for his mates."

Hein has seen and played against the immortals of modern day football. He thinks Cliff Battles was the greatest runner . . . Bronko Nagurski the most rugged straightaway runner . . . Dutch Clark the best field general . . . and Sammy Baugh and Benny Friedman the greatest of the forward passers.

MEL HEIN
Chicago Bears 23, New York Giants 21.
NATIONAL LEAGUE CHAMPIONSHIP, CHICAGO, DECEMBER 17, 1933.

There's one game I'll never forget, a 1933 battle between the Giants and Bears. Though the game was for the National League championship and there were very many memorable occurrences that day, one particular play stands out in my mind as though it happened yesterday.

Besides the added incentive of the title, this was one game the Bears wanted to win. Earlier, in November, we had whipped them, 3 to 0, on a field goal by Ken Strong. Going into the championship encounter, the Bears had been unbeaten since we had defeated them. Nothing, therefore, would've given Bronko Nagurski, Red Grange, Keith Molesworth, etc., more pleasure than to knock off the New York Giants.

It was one of the roughest and toughest games in which I've ever played. And a close one, as the 23-21 score indicates. We threw everything we knew at each other in a wide-open display of offensive trickery. I had a great chance to be a hero on a tricky maneuver but failed because of overanxiety as I stood face-to-face with glory.

On this play, the Giants lined up single wing to the right, with only one man—our end—on my left. On a signal from quarterback Harry Newman, the left end jumped back a yard and our right half-back, Dale Burnett, shifted into the line. This placed me on the end and made me eligible for a pass.

The "pass" was executed by me handing the ball through my legs to Newman, who was up close like a T-quarterback, and he giving it right back to me. Newman then faked having the ball by spinning around and fading back as if to pass. Harry automatically tripped himself and fell on his stomach, whereupon the unsuspecting Bear guards rushed in and dropped on him, thinking he had the ball.

My job, meanwhile, was to walk in a doubled-up position, with the ball tucked in my stomach, until I got well past the backers-up. I was supposed to give our ends a chance to fake a block on the

Courtesy of Jack Tanzer

One of the game's standout centers—Mel Hein.

opposing tackles and then come down to get ahead of me and take out a back who might've gotten wise.

After walking eight yards, the field ahead looked like a lot of invitingly open territory to me. I didn't bother to wait for the ends to move up but started running full speed. The Bears' safety man, Molesworth, caught on and started for me. Not having the ability of a Tuffy Leemans to give an opponent a leg and take it away, I was tackled about 15 yards from a touchdown after gaining about 30. We never did get the ball over on that sequence and it proved the difference later.

To make my embarrassment for not scoring even greater, though, I took a verbal beating from Ray Flaherty and Red Badgro. They were the two ends who vainly tried to get ahead of me and take out Molesworth.

How important that touchdown would have been is emphasized by the course of the game and the final score. You see, it had been ding-dong all the way.

Six times the lead changed hands. Automatic Jack Manders gave the Bears a 3-0 lead in the opening period with the first of three field goals, a boot from the 16. Manders made it 6 to 0 with a 40-yarder in the second quarter before Kink Richards ran 30 yards and Newman passed 39 to Badgro for a 7-6 Giants' edge. It almost was wiped out just before halftime when Grange sprinted 17 yards around end to set up a field goal try which Manders missed from the nine.

Manders didn't miss, though, when Gene Ronzani raced for 15 yards and Carl Brumbaugh took Molesworth's pass to the Giants' 13 early in the third quarter. Jack dropped back to the 19 and put the Bears ahead, 9 to 7. But Newman started flinging passes like pennies in an arcade, hitting Burnett, Richards and Krause to put the ball on the one, from where Krause ended the 61-yard drive with a touchdown plunge.

Back bounced the Bears to regain the lead at 16 to 14 as the game entered the last quarter. A 67-yard pass play, Corbett to Brumbaugh, placed the ball on the eight whereupon, on third down, Nagurski unleashed his famous fake-buck, jump-pass over the line to Karr in the end zone.

We marched 74 yards with the ensuing kickoff, behind Newman's sensational passing, to take a 21-16 lead. That touchdown was scored by a display of brilliant and spontaneous thinking that probably will never have its equal. The play started out as an ordinary reverse from the Bears' 25, with Strong sweeping across from his left half post to take a reverse from Newman. Ken headed for the sideline, found himself trapped and turned and flipped a lateral to Newman, who had been trailing the play.

Now, Harry started back for the other sideline, only to be hemmed in. So, back again he came, frantically trying to figure out what to do with the ball. Suddenly he spied Strong standing alone in the end zone and let fly a pass. Ken leaped, grabbed the ball in the extreme corner and almost fell into the close-by baseball dugout.

That storybook touchdown gave us a 21-16 lead, a seemingly safe one in the comparative few moments that remained. But the Bears roared downfield and, before we knew it, they were on about our 35. We knew what was coming, the same Nagurski fake-buck, jump-pass which gave the Bears their last touchdown. We were ready. But Bronko hit Hewitt with the ball and the latter lateraled to his other end, Karr, who ran the remaining 25 yards or so for what turned out to be the winning score.

There was time for a few more plays and, believe-it-or-not, I had another chance to be a hero. This time, however, it was not my fault the plan didn't work. We were on around our 40 with a very few seconds left when Newman called on the second tricky play we'd rehearsed for a spot such as this. It was the same kind of a formation as before, in which I wound up as an end eligible for a pass.

On this play, however, I snapped the ball to Newman, who fired a lateral to Burnett out on the right. Meantime, I sneaked down along the opposite sideline and was standing all alone on the Bears' 30. Just as Burnett started to throw a pass to me, though, the ball slipped and sailed like a high, lazy punt. A fast pass would've gotten to me in time to get away for possibly a touchdown, or, at least, for enough yardage to enable Strong to try a field goal. However, the lofty aerial gave Molesworth a chance to come over and just knock the ball down.

The game ended one play later. And so did my opportunity to be a hero. So you see what one touchdown—my touchdown—would've meant.

The lineup:
NEW YORK
   (21)   pos.   CHICAGO (23)
Badgro ....le........ Hewitt
Grant ....lt........ Lyman
Gibson ....lg........ Carlson
Hein ....c......... Miller
Jones ....rg........ Kopcha
Owen ....rt........ Musso
Flaherty ....re........ Karr
Newman ....qb........ Brumbaugh
Strong ....lh........ Molesworth
Burnett ....rh........ Ronzani
Molenda ....fb........ Nagurski

New York .... 0—7—7—7——21
Chicago .... 3—3—10—7——23

Touchdowns: *Chicago*—Karr 2, Krause. *New York*—Badgro,
   Strong.

Points after touchdowns: *New York*—Strong 3. *Chicago*—Brumbaugh, Manders.

Field goals: *Chicago*—Manders 3.

Substitutions: *Giants*—Richards, Krause, Irwin, Clancy, Campbell. *Bears*—Manders, Grange, Corbett, Sisk, Pearson, Stahl-
   man.

Referee—Tommy Hughitt, Buffalo. Umpire—Bobby Cahn, Chicago. Field Judge—Robert Karch, Columbia. Head Linesman
   —Dan Tehan, Cincinnati.

ARNOLD CHARLES (ARNIE) HERBER
(*Wisconsin and St. Regis College, Denver*)
GREEN BAY PACKERS, 1932-1940.
NEW YORK GIANTS, 1944-1945.

"*Bingo*" *was the nickname for Arnie Herber, who in eleven years of National Football League competition ranked among the tops in forward passers.*

The De Pere, Wisconsin sharpshooter led the league in passing in 1932, 1934 and 1936. Gifted with a powerful arm, he could throw a ball enormous distances. He could also run a bit, as he demonstrated against Stapleton in 1932, when he not only completed nine of eleven passes, three for touchdowns, but raced 85 and 45 yards for scores himself. The following year, against the Southern California All-Stars, he further showed his versatility by punting 65, 70, 85 and 75 yards in succession and completing three passes for touchdowns.

Herber was a "natural" for Green Bay because he was born there on April 2, 1910. He played little college football—his entire athletic career at both Wisconsin and St. Regis covering only one year—but when he departed from Green Bay at the end of the 1940 season, and four years later made his brief comeback with the Giants, he left an enviable record behind him. And there are many who claim that Herber at his peak was the equal of any forward passer in the game. As for his punting, of which he says little, it is remarkable that the only kick he got off for the Giants during the entire 1945 season covered a distance of 51 yards, second longest kick by anyone that year.

In 11 years, Herber completed 66 touchdown passes and gained 7943 yards with his heaves—a mark bettered only by the great Sammy Baugh and the mighty Sid Luckman.

ARNIE HERBER
New York Giants 28, Philadelphia Eagles 21.
NEW YORK, DECEMBER 2, 1945.

To be able to throw four touchdown passes in the last half and beat the Philadelphia Eagles, 28 to 21, is a thrill that hardly can be matched for me. This took place for me when I was 35 years old and had been in the National League since 1932. When you get old and past your prime, to have a good day—any kind of a good day—is a memorable thing in a player's life. What you do in your prime you expect of yourself but days that come at the end of the trail provide unexpected thrills whenever you think of them. This is beyond question my greatest day in football.

There were other reasons, other than personal, why it was thrilling. The Giants wanted this victory badly. They were going nowhere in particular with a miserable record of only two wins and five defeats. A win at home would at least give the loyal Giant fans some hope for next season. And this was the day on which plaques were unveiled on the center field wall commemorating the deaths of Al Blozis and Jack Lummus, former Giants who gave up their lives during the war. This ball game was for them, too.

I was just another guy on the bench, partly because of a week-long injury and perhaps because there were others, younger and stronger, during a dismal first half in which the Eagles—or rather

Steve Van Buren—buried us under a 14-0 barrage. That big, bruising back from Louisiana State really tore our line to shreds in an Eagle attack that stuck strictly to ground warfare.

In the first period, the Eagles took the ball on their 21 and pounded our forward wall through a 79-yard advance. Van Buren banged over from four yards out. And it was Van Buren again from four yards out who brought the score to 14 to 0 at the half. This time they traveled only 44 yards for the touchdown, but the way that Van Buren was going it seemed as though they could march 1000 yards without our stopping him.

When Van Buren opened the second half by taking the kickoff and galloping 98 yards for his third touchdown and a 21-0 lead, you wouldn't have given an old scorecard for the Giant chances.

It was really a beautiful kickoff return by Jack Doolan from our three to midfield that supplied the spark for one of the greatest comebacks a team ever made. That it was made against an eleven that had to win this game in order to remain in the running for the Eastern Division crown is another testimonial to the Giants that day.

I was truly surprised when Steve Owen called for me at this point in the third period. I'd been aching to get in the game, my first in a couple of weeks, but so little hope as we fell further behind. But Owen, one of the game's keenest strategists, sent me in with definite passing instructions designed to take advantage of weaknesses he had spotted.

In seven minutes, yes seven minutes, we got three touchdowns and tied the score at 21 to 21, but it took great pass-receiving by Frank Liebel to accomplish the almost unheard of feat—the Giant end grabbing three straight touchdown passes.

After Doolan's run, four plays brought the first score. The payoff was my 30-yard pass to Liebel, who took the ball on the eight and carried Van Buren on his back as he crossed the line. One and a half minutes later, Liebel leaped and grabbed a 26-yard pass out of Van Buren's arms on the 15 and we had a second touchdown. Then Liebel, a converted back, snared a nine-yard pass three minutes later and outran the Eagle defense on a 45-yard dash that enabled Ken Strong's third conversion to tie the score.

The game wasn't won yet. The clincher was added by end Sam Fox, who had helped set up Liebel's second touchdown by recovering Van Buren's fumble on our 49. With five minutes left in the game,

Fox stepped into the end zone, turned and caught my spot-pass for the game-winning score.

The Eagles roared back to our four-yard line before the final gun but that's as far as they got. They suffered a defeat from which they never recovered and the Washington Redskins went on to win the Eastern Division title.

Having pitched to ends like Don Hutson, and with him you can't go any further for greatness, I can safely say that Liebel that day was as great an end as ever caught a pass. No finer last chapter could have been written for my football career—that day I came off the bench to help the Giants beat the Eagles.

The lineup:
NEW YORK

(28)	pos.	PHILADELPHIA (21)
Poole	le	Cabrelli
DeFillipo	lt	Sears
Visnic	lg	Michaels
Hein	c	Lindskog
Grate	rg	Banducci
Ragazzo	rt	Wistert
Weiss	re	Humbert
Petrilas	qb	Zimmerman
Livingston	lh	Van Buren
Strong	rh	Steele
Filipowicz	fb	Kish

New York .... 0—0—21—7——28
Philadelphia .... 7—7—7—0——21

Touchdowns: *New York*—Liebel (sub for Poole) 3, Fox (sub for Weiss). *Philadelphia*—Van Buren, 3.

Points after touchdowns: *New York*—Strong, 4. *Philadelphia*—Zimmerman, 3.

Substitutions: *Giants*—Cuff, Sulaitis, Hovious, Paschal, Shaffer, Franck, Doolan, Herber, Liebel, Fox, Springer, Cope, Pederson, Umont, Adams. *Eagles*—Hinkle, Castiglia, Sherman, Thompson, Rogalia, Steinke, McDonald, Ferrante, Mayer, Fritts, Shires, Canale, Kilroy, Maronic, Suffridge, Manzini.

Referee—Roland J. Gibbs, Umpire, John B. Kelly. Field Judge —Charles A. Sweeney. Linesman—Louis J. Gordon.

WILLIAM CLARKE HINKLE
(Bucknell, '32)
GREEN BAY PACKERS, 1932-1941.

No history of football is complete without a chapter on Clarke Hinkle, one of the great fullbacks of our time.

The record books sing his praises as a runner but Hinkle could do everything with a football. He was a great college passer and kicker. His exploits as a runner, however, overshadowed his other talents.

Hinkle was an unnamed All-America in college because Bucknell was too small a school to attain national recognition but his feat of scoring 50 points in three quarters against Dickinson College in 1929 was a brilliant achievement. He led the nation that year in scoring with 122 points. He topped an amazing college record by stealing the show in the annual East-West game in 1932.

At Green Bay, where he played for ten years, Hinkle was always a threat. He didn't have to do any passing with such fine passers as Arnie Herber and Cecil Isbell around, but he did do everything else. He stands fourth in the league records in scoring with 367 points on 42 touchdowns, 31 extra points and 28 field goals. He holds the league standard for the number of running attempts—1171—and he led the league in scoring with 58 points in 1938.

Hinkle was a standout in an era of many great football players and it is a tribute to his ability to be named all-league fullback in 1936, 1937 and 1938. Shifty and fast, he was an elusive target in a broken field. He ran a kickoff 94 yards for a touchdown against the Chicago Bears in 1933.

The debate, of course, will never end as to who is the greatest fullback of all time but Hinkle's name will always be among those of Bronko Nagurski, Ernie Nevers and company.

CLARKE HINKLE
Chicago Bears 24, Green Bay Packers 10.
GREEN BAY, WIS., SEPTEMBER 23, 1934.

If I chose a game in which the Packers were beaten, 24 to 10, you'll probably wonder why that should have been my own greatest day in football. Possibly, more appropriately, I should call it my greatest thrill but we'll settle and call it my most memorable day. That's one day I'll never forget—the time that the mighty Bronko Nagurski and I met in a head-on collision in Green Bay during the Packer-Bear game.

I doubt if we'll ever see another fullback like the Bronk. Here was a man who stood 6 feet, 1 inch in height, weighed 235 pounds and was as fast, if not faster, than most backfield men. He could and had played tackle, guard and end but I remember this tough, rough Minnesotan in the fullback slot. Power, spirit and agility combined to make him a fearful weapon on any gridiron. He didn't run around or over an opponent. He ran right through him.

There's no need to go into the detailed exploits of the man who is virtually unanimously picked as the greatest fullback of all-time. It was a thrill to play against him, although most of the time you wished you were on his side. Green Bay wished just that in this particular game although it was no disgrace to lose to the Bears that year. They won 13 games and were unbeaten until they met the Giants for the world championship.

Clark Hinkle, Green Bay's famous back.

My "meeting" with the Bronko occurred late in the game—too late to do Green Bay any good in the winning columns. I was carrying the ball and Nagurski roared at me to make the tackle. Wham! We banged into each other. Nagurski had to be removed from the game with a broken nose and two closed eyes. Strangely enough, I suffered no ill effects and was able to continue the game. This is one of the rare instances on record where Nagurski came out second best in a football collision. I am no midget myself but I looked like one next to that powerhouse called Nagurski.

The incident was just a little satisfaction for what Nagurski did to us that day. Ripping our line apart like a wild bull, Bronko scored two of his team's three touchdowns and passed to Bill Hewitt for the other when we closed in our defense expecting him on one of his line-smashing rampages.

We had tried desperately to overcome the severe handicap we were forced to work under with the Bronk on the field. Twice, in fact, we fought from behind to tie the score. After Automatic Jack Manders' first-period field goal, Bob Monnett knotted the score at 3-all with a second-period placement. We traded touchdowns in the third quarter, going into the final period all tied at 10 to 10. But Nagurski settled it.

Three weeks later, in Chicago, the Bronko and I "met" again. I had the ball and again he came at me to make the tackle. I felt like a bolt of thunder had just hit me and flew back ten feet but, miraculously, I held my feet and ran 56 yards for a touchdown. Actually, his terrific tackle threw me into the clear, giving me a good start for the touchdown run. They beat us, 27 to 14, that game, and a third time that season, 10 to 6, but personally, I felt good over the unforgettable Nagurski incidents. You can't run into a guy like Nagurski and not remember it.

Lest I create the wrong impression, however, I want to make it clear that Nagurski was as clean a player as you'll ever see. He was liked, feared and respected by all who played against and with him. What pleased me, and you can't exactly blame me, was being able to come off best against the greatest fullback of all time.

That's why I call it my most memorable day or days in football. I'd have to choose it, although you might not, over the day in 1929 when I scored 50 points for Bucknell against Dickinson College to become high scorer of the country. You think I'm crazy, eh? Brother, you've never run into Nagurski!

The lineup:
CHICAGO
(21)   pos.   GREEN BAY (10)
Hewitt .... le .... Gantenbein
Lyman .... lt .... Jorgensen
Carlson .... lg .... Michaleske
Kawal .... c .... Bultman
Kopcha .... rg .... Jones
Musso .... rt .... Kurth
Karr .... re .... Norgard
Brumbaugh .... qb .... Goldenberg
Feathers ...... lh .... Monnett
Ronzani ...... rh .... Grove
Nagurski ...... fb .... Hinkle
Chicago .... 3—0—7—14——21
Green Bay .... 0—3—7—0——10
Touchdowns: *Bears*—Nagurski, 2, Hewitt. *Packers*—Goldenberg.
Points after touchdowns: *Bears*—Manders, 3. *Packers*—Monnett.
Field Goals: *Bears*—Manders. *Packers*—Monnett.

DON HUTSON
(*Alabama, '35*)
GREEN BAY PACKERS, 1935-1945.

The Alabama Antelope is the greatest pass receiver of all time. That's an unchallenged honor belonging to Don Hutson, who was one of the thrill-makers in the Rose Bowl classic of 1935, and who went on for 11 years as the super-end of the Green Bay Packers and pro football.

Hutson, fresh from his brilliant career at Alabama, caught a touchdown pass on his first play as a professional and the records he proceeded to set up in the ensuing years will take many more to erase. In eight of his 11 years, he was the league's leading pass receiver. For five successive years, 1940 through 1944, he led the league in scoring. He was named most valuable in 1941 and 1942, the only player to be so honored twice. He scored 825 points and romped to 105 touchdowns.

The 190-pound, 6-foot, 1-inch flash who could run 100 yards in 9.7 seconds—a combination of speed and illusiveness sometimes unbelievable—was not only a mighty end but a fine kicker as well. In a league that had such kickers as Jack Manders and Ken Strong, among others, Hutson topped them all with 174 points after touchdown.

When Hutson, after announcing his retirement for three years only to return each year because of the wartime manpower shortage, finally hung up his cleats at the end of the 1945 season, he owned 19 league records. The 19th is for holding the most league records.

An All-America end in 1934, All-League end eight times, the modest flanker from Pine Bluff, Arkansas, who was also a track and baseball star, quietly accepts praise with:

"I had a good day."

There were many of those days for the Antelope.

DON HUTSON
Green Bay 7, Chicago Bears 0.
CHICAGO, SEPTEMBER 15, 1935.

I had a good day in Pasadena's Rose Bowl before a frightening crowd of 85,000 screaming fans. It was a great thrill but I have never been so thrilled nor so frightened as I was by my first meeting with the Chicago Bears.

I was a tall, skinny kid when I came out of Alabama to join the Green Bay Packers and the pros in 1935. Despite my 6 feet plus 1 inch in height, I looked like a side of a goal post standing beside the giant frames of the Cal Hubbards, the George Mussos, the Ernie Smiths and the other bruising behemoths. Maybe that's one reason Coach Curly Lambeau let me sit out the National League opener against the Chicago Cardinals the previous week. He kept me from the Cardinals to toss me to the Bears.

The Bears were arch rivals of Green Bay and what a ferocious lot they were then, even as now. For three successive years they had been the virtual class of the league. In 1932, before the league had been divided into Eastern and Western sections, and brought about the playoff system, the Bears won the championship. The next season, with the playoffs, they won again, and in the fabulous season of 1934, while I was catching Dixie Howell's passes at Alabama, they roared through 13 straight wins before losing to the Giants in the now historic "Basketball Shoes" playoff.

That was the background of the team I was asked to face in my professional debut. Not only that, but Green Bay hadn't beaten the Bears since 1932, going down to defeat seven times in a row. I not only had to play a great team but fight a "jinx" as well. I admit I was a little bit shaky as we lined up to receive the kickoff.

Hank Bruder, our fullback, took the boot in the end zone and raced it out to the 17 where he was completely snowed under by angry Bears. Then Arnie Herber, he of the strong and accurate arm, hit the unsuspecting Bear defense with a bombshell. He took the center snap, faded back near the goal line and let fly one of his famous specialties—a long, floating pass that seemed to hang invitingly in mid-air. The Bears never expected a pass from deep in our own territory and were completely off balance for the play. I was able to race out into the clear all alone, grab the perfect 50-yard throw and speed away to a touchdown.

A touchdown on my first play in pro football. And a touchdown that was the only one in the game, too, enabling us to upset mighty Chicago, 7 to 0.

This was the top day of many days to come. I've been lucky. I've always had a great passer on the pitching end. At Alabama it was Howell. At Green Bay, it was first Herber, then the unpredictable Cecil Isbell, now coach of the Baltimore Colts.

Isbell was as great a halfback as the National League ever had. On one occasion, in the Pro Bowl game of 1939, in Los Angeles, Isbell grabbed my ear and whispered his plan delightedly. We were on our own two-yard line at the time and the play was so fantastic I had no choice but to grin and accept. I broke fast and raced away as Cece threw the ball 69 yards through the California air. I caught it for a touchdown that covered a total of 108 yards.

We also hold the record for the shortest completed pass—a pass that almost led Lambeau to early retirement. We were playing the Cleveland Rams on October 8, 1942. It was first down for Green Bay on their four-inch line. Get that—first down and only four inches to smash over. The Rams set for the inevitable drive—but that never came. Isbell took the ball, whirled and threw to me in the end zone for a touchdown.

Lambeau was weak and pale. He rushed Isbell back to the bench. "Cece," he groaned, "don't ever do that again. Don't ever do that again."

Of course, Isbell had an explanation. If he missed, he still had three other chances to smash away for the four inches.

These and other plays and days all brought thrills . . . thrills like playing on the Green Bay world's champions of 1936, 1939 and 1944 . . . being honored with two Most Valuable Player Awards . . . scoring one or more points in 41 straight games . . . my long association with Curly Lambeau.

Thrills? Plenty of them. But none like my first professional football game.

The lineup:

GREEN BAY (7)	pos.	CHICAGO BEARS (0)
Hutson	le	Hewitt
Hubbard	lt	Buss
Michalske	lg	Carlson
Butler	c	Kawal
Kiesling	rg	Kopcha
Schwammel	rt	Musso
Gantenbein	re	Karr
Goldenberg	qb	Masterson
Herber	lh	Feathers
Blood	rh	Ronzani
Bruder	fb	Manders

Green Bay .... 7—0—0—0——7
Chicago .... 0—0—0—0——0

Touchdown: *Packers*—Hutson.

Point after Touchdown: *Packers*—Monnett.

Substitutions: *Bears*—Johnson, Crawford, Trost, Rosequist, Zeller, McPherson, H. Miller, Richards, O. Miller, Pollock, Molesworth, Corbett, Sisk, Grosvenor, Dunlap. *Green Bay*—Vairo, Tenner, Rose, Seibold, Smith, Perry, O'Connor, Engebretson, Evans, Svendsen, Barrager, Monnett, Schneidman, Grove, Johnson, Sauer, Laws, Hinkle.

FRANCIS WILLIAM (FRANK) LEAHY
(Notre Dame, '31)
GEORGETOWN, 1931.
MICHIGAN STATE, 1932.
FORDHAM, 1933-1938.
BOSTON COLLEGE, 1939-1940.
NOTRE DAME, 1941-1943; 1946-   .

"Material, coaching, blocking and tackling—not systems—win football games. A team that can win them all with the Notre Dame system can win them all with any other system, everything else being equal."

That's the wisdom of Frank Leahy, head man at Notre Dame, and he has gone quietly about his way to prove it over the years. After seven years of coaching apprenticeship as a line coach at Georgetown, Michigan State, and Fordham, Leahy moved to the top coaching spot at Boston College and produced a two-year record of 20 wins in 22 games. He crowned that achievement with the Eagles' 19-13 victory over Tennessee in the Sugar Bowl at New Orleans, in 1941.

When Notre Dame was looking around for a coach to replace Elmer Layden, "The Thin Man," they finally decided on Leahy. At Notre Dame, Leahy might have become a great tackle but a knee injury hampered his activity and he spent a good deal of his time helping Rockne with the line and absorbing the teachings of the "master of coaches" and his assistants.

Leahy's record at Notre Dame is phenomenal. In five years, which includes the unbeaten and untied season of 1947, the Irish have captured 41 games, lost three and were tied four times. In 1943, 1946 and 1947, they gained recognition as national champions. He has received three awards as Coach of the Year, and his ability as a coach and speaker has put him in great demand for lectures at countless coaching schools.

Two years in the Navy did not seem to dull the Irish mentor's "football brains." His departure was only a brief reprieve for opposing colleges. The cry of "Break Up Notre Dame" will be heard as long as Leahy is around to coach the Ramblers.

FRANK LEAHY
FEBRUARY 15, 1941.

The most memorable incident of my football career occurred when I received the opportunity to return to my alma mater, Notre Dame, as head football coach and athletic director. If you've ever played football, or any sport, for that matter, you can appreciate the thrill I got and still get when I think back to the day I was asked to come home and take charge of Notre Dame's football fortunes.

Imagine. To handle a coaching job that once was in the hands of the immortal Knute Rockne is a thrill in itself, but to a Notre Dame man there could be nothing more thrilling than coaching football at Notre Dame. If I seem to go on and on, I'm sure it's understandable.

I often think back to that February day in 1941 when I strolled along the Notre Dame campus; familiar to me in my undergraduate days but, then, cloaked in unprecedented splendor as I glowingly headed for the office of Father J..Hugh O'Donnell, C.S.C., president of Notre Dame.

I'm a bit ahead of the story, though. In fact, about a month. It all started early in January, 1941, after Boston College had defeated Tennessee, 19 to 13, in the New Year's Day Sugar Bowl game.

I was riding the waves of good luck in my second year as a head coach and quickly was offered a number of opportunities to change jobs—two being coaching positions. At the same time, Boston College's graduate manager of athletics, John Curley, was after me to sign a new contract he'd offered in the middle of the season.

Frank Leahy signs as Coach and Athletic Director of Notre Dame in the presence of The Rev. J. Hugh O'Donnell, C.S.C., its president in 1941.

Actually, I wasn't interested in changing my job, so that eliminated all outside offers. Where the Boston College contract was concerned, I wasn't satisfied with the terms tendered my assistants— Johnny Druze, Ed McKeever and Joe McArdle.

Curley adjusted their terms, but I still didn't sign. There was no particular reason why I didn't heed his pleas, other than I just wasn't in a hurry or mood to okay the contract. That is, until Curley got me in his office one day and, in the presence of McKeever and Bill Sullivan, director of publicity, pinned me down.

Just before I signed the contract, Curley turned to me and said:

"If Notre Dame ever asks you back, Frank, we'll be happy to hand you your release."

It was just a spontaneous remark. Little did he or I know, at the time, that Boston College would have the opportunity to live up to the statement a little less than two weeks later.

About a week later, the announcement came that Elmer Layden had quit Notre Dame to accept a five-year contract as president of the National Football League. Immediately my name appeared on a list of potential successors that included Clipper Smith, of Villanova; Jim Crowley, whom I had assisted at Fordham and who recommended me for the Boston College job; Buck Shaw, of Santa Clara; Harry Stuhldreher, of Wisconsin; Frank Thomas, of Alabama; Gus Dorais, of Detriot, and many more former Notre Dame men.

I felt that everybody mentioned was more qualified for the job than myself. Still, I kept hoping that somehow, some way I'd get it. Along with hoping, I further kindled my optimism by repeating to myself:

"Should Notre Dame consider me for the job, the way at least has been prepared for my release by Mr. Curley's statement just before I re-signed with Boston College."

Within another week, the phone rang in my Waban, Mass., home. It was then, with that call, that I was offered the position of athletic director and head football coach of Notre Dame . . . provided I wanted the job and were free to take it.

By appointment, arrangements were made for a meeting with Rev. Frank Cavanaugh, C.S.C., in Albany, N. Y. At the conference, I told him I would want to bring along Druze, McKeever and McArdle as my assistants. This was okayed on the part of Notre Dame. All I needed was an official release from Boston College, now.

A few days passed and, on February 15, I was back on the Notre Dame campus. In my pocket I carried a letter of release from Rev. Francis Murphy, S.J., president of Boston College. I headed straight for the office of Rev. O'Donnell and signed the contract which entrusted to me the great honor of coaching the Fighting Irish.

That was my greatest day in football.

LOUIS (LOU) LITTLE
(*Pennsylvania, '20*)
PHILADELPHIA YELLOW JACKETS, 1921-1923.
GEORGETOWN, 1924-1929.
COLUMBIA, 1930-   .

It was only fitting that Lou Little, who missed going to the Rose Bowl with Penn in 1917 because he enlisted in the Army, should eventually lead a team into Pasadena. Molding Columbia's 1933 team into a resourceful, alert machine that went on to score one of the greatest upsets in Rose Bowl history is just one of Little's many accomplishments.

Little has been a powerful man in collegiate football history since giving up a three-year player-coach career with the professional Philadelphia Yellow Jackets in 1924. He has been active with the rules and advisory committees for many years and his contributions to football justly were recognized when he was given the New York Touchdown Club Award in 1943. The trophy goes annually to the "one who has done the most towards the advancement of the game and who has made some contribution of permanent value."

At Georgetown, his teams won 41, lost nine and tied twice. And it was while at the Washington, D. C., school that a Little-coached team first gained the headlines when the Hoyas upset a heavily favored Ken Strong and Al Lassman-led NYU team in the Yankee Stadium, 2 to 0. Moving to Columbia, Lou became an immediate success where, in his first five seasons, the Lions won 34, lost eight and tied two.

The quiet, modest Little, who matriculated at Vermont and then switched to Penn where he became a great tackle, is famous for his coaching abilities. Never blessed with an overflow of material comparable to the major colleges Columbia plays, Lou still manages to turn out winning teams. It's a tribute to his ability to pass on knowledge of fundamentals that Columbia has become famous for its long line of great quarterbacks—Ralph Hewitt, Cliff Montgomery, Sid Luckman, Paul Governali and Gene Rossides.

LOU LITTLE
Columbia 7, Stanford 0.
ROSE BOWL, JANUARY 1, 1934.

We were on our way back from Pasadena where the Columbia football team had astounded the nation by upsetting a powerhouse Stanford eleven, 7 to 0, in the Rose Bowl. The train was a special and we made our way leisurely across the country, stopping here and there to appear before alumni groups.

Pulling into an unscheduled Nebraska whistlestop to fill the train's water tanks, we were amazed to see a crowd of about 250 people in the station. Some of us got off to stretch our legs and the people quickly smothered us with congratulations. Suddenly, a little, old woman pushed her way forward.

"Mr. Little," she said. "Here's a nice, big chocolate cake for you and your players. I have three boys and I know what a home-baked chocolate cake would mean to them if they were far from home."

That little gesture by that kindly woman is the reason I'll always rate Columbia's 1934 Rose Bowl victory my greatest day in football. It's simple. There was a woman, from a small Nebraska town, who undoubtedly never knew that Columbia had a football team until we beat Stanford. With that one victory we put Columbia on the gridiron map . . . made it the most talked of eleven in the country.

That's why I've chosen the Rose Bowl triumph over Columbia's stupendous upset of Army in 1947, which ended the West Point three-year winning streak. When we played the Cadets, it was a battle of two major football teams. However, when we received the invitation to play Stanford in the Tournament of Roses classic, it was heralded as a game between the country's No. 1 team—Stanford —and "a high school eleven"—that was supposed to be Columbia.

Some people were more surprised over Columbia getting the invitation to play than its victory. Out in California, they boasted that many Coast high school elevens were larger than Columbia's squad. And here in the East . . . well, there was no more surprised man than Mr. Lou Little. In fact, I thought the whole thing a gag at first.

I had heard that unbeaten Princeton, which had whipped us earlier in the season, had the inside track. So when Al Masters, Stanford's graduate manager of athletics, called my home soon after I'd returned from the Notre Dame-Army game, I figured it was a rib. Masters had a tough time convincing me that the call was legitimate. To be truthful after telling him I'd have to hand his invitation over to Columbia's Board of Trustees, I called the long distance operator and she told me the call had come from Palo Alto.

Lou Little of Columbia, always a top coach.

Naturally, Wild Bill Donovan and the other members of the Board of Trustees gave the trip their okay. Now it was up to the football team. We knew we had a tremendous task before us. Stanford was rated about 25 points better than the Lions. It was a team of All-Americas—Bobby Grayson, who was being likened to Ernie Nevers, Monk Moscrip, Bill Corbus and Bob Reynolds. They had the reputations but we had the determination.

To me, beating Stanford was not an upset. I didn't go to Pasadena to fall, and neither did my boys. I felt all along that we could win and so did they. Right from the start I impressed on the players that we weren't going to California as a bunch of tourists. We were going out for a football game that we could win if they worked. And they worked.

It came as a disappointment to the California people, but we disregarded Rose Bowl custom by not leaving for the Coast until 10 days before the game. I didn't want my players to think they were on a sight-seeing trip. And I didn't want them to lose their edge by attending a flock of pre-game social functions.

So we left New York the day before Christmas and headed for Tucson, Ariz. On the way out, I had the players scramble off the train every day for a short workout. And, when we got to Tucson, the boys really went to work. They drilled harder than any team I ever saw.

Practicing under the broiling Arizona sun, I had them run our favorite KF79 play hundreds of times. We had three check plays, or variations, of KF79 and they all looked alike. I'd stand in front of the boys and tell them to try and fool me. I made them run it over and over until they did. By the time we left a week later everybody knew that Columbia was as ready as it could be, including some Coast sportswriters who had come to our camp for interviews and were amazed when I told them they could watch us drill because I didn't believe in barring newspapermen from practices.

We were in great mental and physical shape when we reached the Coast Sunday morning, the day before the game. I had brought the players along steadily and they were at their peak condition. However, my victory confidence received a sharp setback when we arrived in California simultaneous with a torrential rainstorm.

The well-drained field looked unplayable. There was about 6-7 inches of water along the sidelines. So a hurried conference that

Lou Little, Columbia, with Al Barabas (left) and Capt. Cliff Mont-
gomery holding the trophy after the 1934 Rose Bowl triumph over
Stanford.

Sunday evening was held with the object of postponing the game
until Wednesday, when the day would be proclaimed a public holi-
day. That's what the Rose Bowl officials wanted but not Columbia.

We were scheduled to play on Monday and that's when we were
going to play. We were on edge. As Cliff Montgomery, our quarterback, put it:

"I'd like to play it even if we have to swim."

So Monday it was. And, though the rain turned to a light drizzle
the day of the game, the wet field made passing practically impossible. A tough break for us, because we felt we could pass Stanford to
death. Our reports classified Stanford as a great offensive team but
mediocre on pass defense. Therefore, the slippery football immedi-

ately took away one of our attacking weapons and minimized our victory chances.

We only threw two forward passes but needed only one . . . the one we completed. It led to the game's only touchdown and came in the second period after Alustiza, who had three Lions block his kick on the previous play and saw teammate Reynolds recover, seemingly punted Stanford out of danger. But Montgomery carried the boot to the Indians' 45 and a penalty moved it up another five.

Cliff, on the first play, faded and tossed a pass to Tony Matal. Our end made a leaping catch, came down sliding and finally put us on their 17. Then came the KF79 play, which had just failed to get us a first-period touchdown because safety-man Maentz speedily cut across and pulled Al Barabas down by one ankle 25 yards from a score.

A bit of assignment improvising in the huddle took care of the Maentz threat. Pinckney, our left guard, told left end McDowell to forget about hitting the halfback but to go for Maentz, instead. Ordinarily, we didn't bother with the safety man but Maentz' speed was too great a threat. So, and the pictures showed it clearly, McDowell wiped out Maentz while Pinckney took care of the halfback and Barabas was able to skip for a touchdown untouched.

Just before Barabas ran for the winning score, he fumbled but recovered for a half-yard loss. Then came good old KF79 and the ball game. Here's how it worked, with the blocking help of Pinckney and McDowell:

Montgomery took the ball from center, wheeled in a deceptive maneuver and faked a handoff to right half Brominski, who headed between right tackle and right end, drawing the secondary towards him. Meanwhile, Barabas cut around from left half, took the pigskin from Cliff and, completely fooling everybody by hiding the ball behind his left hip, raced around right end on a naked reverse to score.

As Herb Kopf, one of my assistants that year, said:

"Stanford hasn't seen the ball yet."

But Barabas' touchdown wasn't the only contribution to Columbia's victory. He provided the points; they had to be protected because Stanford, as I said, was a terrific offensive team.

Four times during the second half, they pounded us against our goal line. But our kids, with the aid of only two line substitutions and four in the backfield, stopped them on the one, 14, 20 and then the eight in the fourth quarter. Brominski, Wilder, Ciampa, Nevel, Barabas, etc., refused to allow their goal line to be crossed.

Brominski recovered a fumble on our one. A Grayson bobble stopped Stanford on our 14. A penalty helped us halt them on our 20 and then a fine Barabas tackle ended their final threat on our eight.

The confident, winning spirit that inspired Columbia that day was best exemplified by Brominski's reaction when a group of photographers gathered in back of the end zone and prepared to take pictures of an expected Stanford touchdown during one of its second-half drives. Brominski, with Columbia backed close to its goal line, turned and yelled:

"You guys better get back to midfield. If you start now, you can walk. Otherwise you'll have to run."

The statistics tell a misleading story. They got 16 first downs to our six; netted 272 yards to our 114 and had six scoring chances to our three. But we played strictly defensive football after tallying, I having told the boys to sit tight and not throw any passes unless the score changed. It didn't and we gained the edge in the one statistical department that counts—scoring.

That's the story of a record achievement that'll never be matched. It can't be matched because we're the only Rose Bowl team to be sent on its way by one mayor and welcomed home by another. For, when we left for California John O'Brien was in office and, upon our January return, he had been succeeded by Fiorello LaGuardia.

The lineup:
COLUMBIA

(7)	pos.	STANFORD (0)
McDowell	le	Smith
Jackel	lt	Callaway
Pinckney	lg	Corbus
Wilder	c	Miller
Dzamba	rg	O'Connor
Richavich	rt	Reynolds
Matal	re	Moscrip
Montgomery	qb	Alustiza
Barabas	lh	Hamilton
Brominski	rh	Maentz
Nevel	fb	Grayson

Columbia .... 0—7—0—0——7
Stanford .... 0—0—0—0——0
Touchdown: *Columbia*—Barabas.
Point after touchdown: *Columbia*—Wilder.
Substitutions: *Columbia*—Linehan, Tomb, Chippendale, Chase, Ciampa, Demshar. *Stanford*—Topping, Van Dellen, Drown, Adams, Trompas, Bates, Sim, Hillman.
Referee—Tom Louttit, Oregon State. Umpire—Ed Thorp, De-LaSalle. Head Linesman—W. R. Crowley, Bowdoin. Field Judge—Tom Fitzpatrick, Utah.

SIDNEY (SID) LUCKMAN
(*Columbia, '39*)
CHICAGO BEARS, 1939-   .

Mr. Quarterback!

That's what they call Sid Luckman, "the greatest quarterback to work the T."

The tribute comes not only from George Halas, owner and coach of the Chicago Bears, but from most of football. And few will dispute the statement about the guy who learned his football on the streets of fabulous Brooklyn.

As a high school student at Erasmus, and later at Columbia University under Lou Little, Luckman gained acclaim for his passing wizardry and All-America honors in 1938. Drafted by the Bears in 1939, he moved into his new spot as if it was made to order for him. With Luckman at the master-minding helm, the Bears have won five division titles and four league crowns. He was All-League quarterback in 1941-42-43 and 1944, when the league stopped making selections. He was Most Valuable in 1943. And he holds countless league records.

Sid Luckman ranks with Ralph Hewitt and Cliff Montgomery as the all-time quarterback in Columbia history. Columbia had a mediocre season in 1938 but it was his 82-yard touchdown run against Army that helped the Lions upset the Soldiers, 20 to 18. He completed 66 of 132 passes that year, a sign of the greatness to come. His most coveted record is the one in which he threw seven touchdown passes in a game against the Giants. But, even more indicative of his prowess, is the mark he holds for throwing touchdown passes in 19 consecutive games—three in 1942, 10 in 1943, and six in 1944.

SID LUCKMAN

Chicago Bears 56, New York Giants 7

NEW YORK, NOVEMBER 14, 1943.

Every time a forward passer connects for a touchdown it gives him a thrill. You can almost remember every touchdown pass you've ever thrown. It's the same kind of unforgettable feeling a baseball player gets when he smacks a home run. Well, on November 14, 1943, in the Polo Grounds, I smashed out "seven home runs" and, boy, I'll never forget it or lose the thrill of even telling the story.

Seven touchdown passes I threw that afternoon. When the game, in which we broke six National League records, was over I was hailed for my achievement. But alongside my name in the record books they should list those of Jim Benton, Hampton Pool, Harry Clark, Connie Berry, George Wilson and Co-coaches Luke Johnsos and Hunk Anderson. And while I'm about it, you can add those of Danny Fortmann, Bulldog Turner, George Musso, Gary Famiglietti, Dante Magnani and all the other guys who gave me rock-wall protection.

If the Bears were a perfect team against the Washington Redskins when we handed them that humiliating 73-0 defeat in 1940, they were close to perfect this afternoon. Benton, Pool, Clark, Berry and Wilson were the pass catchers who helped the Bears set other records such as 702 yards gained, another for the 508 yards picked up on passing, and a third for seven scoring passes. Bob Snyder made eight conversions for another mark. My passing produced 453 yards, a new standard for a single game, and, of course, there were those seven touchdowns by a single passer. Actually, however, Johnsos and Anderson were the most important figures in the record-breaking festivities as far as I'm concerned.

First of all, it was they who sensed I was near the six-touchdown record of Sammy Baugh. And it was they who kept sending me back into the ball game, already safely won, when I could have been kept on the bench and saved for the following week's tough game with unbeaten Washington.

The Giants were the unfortunate victims of the Bears' lust for records that afternoon. When it was over, we had handed Steve Owen's boys their worst defeat in National League history—a 56-7 shellacking. They didn't lay down, though. In fact, it took some great pass-catching by our fellows to outdo their stubborn defense. You never walk over a Steve Owen team—you always know you've been in a fight.

Sid Luckman approves Bear contract, 1939, with owner-coach George Halas.

They held us off early in the first period, after Clark took a 30-yard pass and ran 18 with it. But midway in the quarter, Benton grabbed a 19-yard toss and raced 35 along the sidelines to the Giants' eight. We got the first touchdown on fourth down when Benton snared a pass in the coffin corner.

The second one came on the last play of the period. We were 54 yards away from pay dirt when, behind perfect protection that the Giants couldn't penetrate even with the aid of dynamite, I let fly a long one. Berry outraced the secondary to take it on the 28 and went the rest of the way.

Thereafter, we kept up a two-touchdown-a-quarter pace. I just threw them and always there was a Bear around to catch the ball. They seemed to have glued fingers. The Giants had marched 73 yards to a score, when we came back with an 89-yard drive that ended with Pool taking a 27-yard touchdown heave on fourth down. Then, to show them that we could travel on the ground, too, we battered 60 yards to No. 4, aided by a 31-yard sprint by Magnani and Clark's four-yard smash over. That was the only score we made that wasn't on a pass.

Shortly after the second half began, we covered 78 yards and tallied on a sensational catch by Clark. The payoff play started on the Giants' 38. I tossed one long and down the middle. The ball headed straight for the goal posts but just as it seemed ready to strike, Clark leaped and picked it out of the air.

There was no stopping the Bears. The next parade covered 76 yards and got Benton his second touchdown on a pass from the Giants' 15. A Tuffy Leemans fumble resulted in another six-pointer, this time on a heave to Wilson from three yards out.

The Giants never gave up but they couldn't stem the tide of a fateful afternoon for us. We took the ball on our 20, and they rushed me back into the ball game. My orders were to pass and nothing else.

I passed. The first one went 40 yards to Ray McLean to put the ball on the Giants' 40. Then came a 37-yard heave to Pool, who battled two Giants for the ball on the three, gained possession and staggered the remaining yardage before toppling into the end zone.

Thus did I enjoy my greatest day. The fact that I defeated an accepted sports theory, further enhanced my thrill. Before the game that day, I received a $1000 war bond from my hometown Brooklyn rooters and another from my teammates. An athlete "honored" on his day is supposed to be "jinxed" in sports. When I wasn't handling that ball, I kept my fingers crossed against the jinx. You can't pass without your fingers crossed.

The lineup:

CHICAGO (56)	pos.	NEW YORK (7)
Benton	le	Adams
Steinkemper	lt	Cope
Fortmann	lg	Younce
Turner	c	Hein
Musso	rg	Avedesian
Hoptowit	rt	Blozis
Wilson	re	Walls
Luckman	qb	Shaffer
Clark	lh	Nix
Magnani	rh	Cuff
Famiglietti	fb	Kinscherf

Chicago .... 14—14—14—14——56
New York .... 0—7—0—0——7

Touchdowns: *Chicago*—Benton, 2, Pool, 2, Clark, 2, Berry, Wilson. *New York*—Kinscherf.

Point after touchdowns: *Chicago*—Snyder, 8. *New York*—Cuff.

Substitutions: *Bears*—Berry, Pool, Nagurski, Sigillo, Babartsky, Gridauskas, Logan, Ippolito, Matuza, Mundee, Snyder, Nolting, McEnulty, McLean, Masters. *Giants*—Pritko, Liebel, Carroll, Visnic, Marone, Roberts, Dubzinski, Piccolo, Leemans, Brown, Trocolor, Sulaitis, Karcis, Paschal.

Referee—Carl Rebele. Umpire—Harry Robb. Field Judge—Eugene Miller. Linesman—Charley Berry.

DR. WILLIAM T. (BULLET BILL) OSMANSKI, D.D.S.

(Holy Cross, '39)

IOWA, 1939.
CHICAGO BEARS, 1939-1942.
GREAT LAKES, 1943.
CAMP LEJEUNE, 1945.
CHICAGO BEARS, 1945-1947.
HOLY CROSS, 1948- .

It has been said that "no ball carrier is a hero to his blocker," and while this epigram may hold more than the proverbial grain of truth, it never applied to Bill Osmanski, D.D.S. Both in college, where he was virtually a one-man backfield on more than one occasion, and in the pro ranks, Osmanski was a "ball players' player." Everybody likes this big, bruising fullback with the sense of humor—even the opposition.

Osmanski is regarded as one of the greatest products of Holy Cross football. A sensation as a freshman, he roared right on with the varsity until he reached unquestioned All-America heights in 1938.

He was a brilliant, plunging fullback in the All-Star game of 1939, and it was largely due to him that the pro Giants were held to nine points on three field goals. He proved he could play football with anybody when he joined the Bears that same year and promptly won not only All-League fullback honors but led the ground-gainers with 699 yards gained in 121 attempts.

Some of Osmanski's college exploits included runs of 85, 67, 65, 45 and 92 yards. It was his 72-yard run off tackle on the second play of the game that started the Bears on their famous 73-0 trouncing of the Washington Redskins for the pro championship in 1940. A great runner—a great team player—undoubtedly a great dentist in between football seasons—Bill Osmanski returns to his beloved Holy Cross as head coach of football and judging by his past performances, he should prove an immediate success.

BILL OSMANSKI
Holy Cross 32, Brown 0.
PROVIDENCE, R. I., NOVEMBER 14, 1936.

My brother Joe, who also did a bit of football playing for the Chicago Bears, and I, were practicing prior to the opening of the training season. Joe threw me a pass—me being a balding athlete—and I ran like the blazes to catch it. I did. A passerby saw the play, strolled over to my little brother and said:

"Your father runs pretty fast for an old man."

For an "old man" there have been many memorable days in football. There was the time I received the Outstanding Player Award in the 1939 All-Star game against the Giants, played before a Soldiers Field crowd of 90,000. Also the time when I tackled Corby Davis, the Cleveland fullback, and knocked two of his teeth out—not premeditated, of course.

That last one was a memorable occurrence because I was in my second year at dental school then, and, being rather interested in teeth, I immediately began giving Corby a clinical examination. While the befuddled referee found it was like pulling teeth trying to get the ball that Davis unconsciously refused to give up, I looked over Corby's mouth and right then and there had him agree to a dental appointment.

There were other unforgettable moments, including the time Fred Allen outjoked me by jesting he knew I was going to be a

Courtesy of Jack Tanzer

Bullet Bill Osmanski, the "ball player's player" turned Holy Cross coach.

dentist because every time I'd hit the line I'd say: "Open up. This won't hurt a bit."

All kidding aside, though, I'd have to go back to my Holy Cross days for my greatest day. That was the day when I scored three touchdowns within 10 minutes against a Brown team we licked, 32 to 0. I was only a sophomore then, so you can imagine how I felt when I twice ran 65 yards for touchdowns and tallied a third on a one-yard plunge. But my success that day boomeranged. Despite the fact I was aching to play more, the coach, Eddie Anderson, benched the regulars for the rest of the game.

However, in the 20 minutes I played there were enough personal thrills to last a lifetime. Of course, we were vastly superior to Brown that season, partcularly our first string line of Shields, Gavin, Carr, Mautner, Luciano, Delaney and O'Donnell. Those fellows never let

Brown into our territory and, in turn, ripped gaping holes in the Bruin forward wall.

It's easy to advance when there's nobody there to stop you. And our line saw to that. It got its first chance when Dougherty's quick-kick, two minutes after the game started, touched the leg of Foster, trying to block out our end, O'Donnell. O'Donnell fell on the ball on the Brown 11 and three plays later the line helped me crack over right tackle from the one.

The score went to 13 to 0 after a Brown punt was downed on our 35. On the first play, one on which we called for an ordinary smash at Brown's left tackle, I broke into daylight and raced the rest of the way untouched.

My third touchdown came early in the second period following Hall's brilliant quick-kick that ended up on our 10. I picked up eight through a big hole in tackle, swept around Brown's blocked out left end for 17, and then took Kidd's lateral to cover the remaining 65 yards.

The rest of the game, even without the regulars, was routine. Against the reserves, Brown managed to reach our five—its only entry into Crusader territory, but a fumble ended that chance. Bartholomeo scored another touchdown for us before the half ended, and Massey raced 70 yards in the final period for the last score.

I've played a lot of football and have seen players who would stand up against the best in any era. Were I to pick an All-Time, All-Star team from the ranks of those I've played against, it would have Don Hutson and George Wilson at the ends, Chester Adams and Joe Stydahar at tackle, Dan Fortmann and Ramsey at guard, Bulldog Turner in the center slot; Sid Luckman at quarter; George McAfee and Steve Van Buren at the halfback posts, and the mighty Bronko Nagurski at fullback.

The lineup:

HOLY CROSS (32)	pos.	BROWN (0)
Shields	le	Petrone
Gavin	lt	Battles
Carr	lg	Carifio
Mautner	c	Turcone
Luciano	rg	Wisback
Delaney	rt	Beaubien

O'Donnell ......re........ Larkowich
Kidd ....qb....... Atwell
Dougherty .....lh........ Foster
Gallogly ....rh........ Ostergard
Osmanski .....fb........ Riegler
Holy Cross ....13—13—0—6——32
Brown .... 0—0—0—0——0

Touchdowns: *Holy Cross*—Osmanski, 3, Bartholomeo, Massey.

Points after touchdowns: *Holy Cross*—Kidd, 2.

Substitutions: *Holy Cross*—Massey, Ouellette, Bartholomeo, Paraskas, LaTanzi, McGuane, Tassimari, Nosek, Collins, Zimti, Ryan, Ritterhaus, O'Melia, Wiley, Manoli. *Brown*—Hall, Vaughan, Bernstein, Kapstein, Pease, Ambrosini, Goodby, Cioci, Sharkey, Battles, Certuse, Saklad, Hawley, Blake, Stanhope.

STEPHEN (STOUT STEVE) OWEN
(*Phillips University, '23*)
KANSAS CITY COWBOYS, 1923-1925.
NEW YORK GIANTS, 1926-   .

Because Phillips University in Enid, Oklahoma, is only a little school, Steve Owen never gained the All-America recognition he deserved. But his college and professional opponents will admit without reluctance that the renowned New York Giants coach was one of the greatest linemen of our time. He since has become an All-America coach.

Finishing his collegiate baseball, wrestling and football careers in 1921, Steve returned to Phillips for one season of line coaching. On the verge of a wrestling career, he accepted an offer to play a pro football game with Tulsa City against Jim Thorpe and the Toledo Maroons.

That was the start of a professional gridiron career that led to three seasons (1923-25) with the Kansas City Cowboys, whereupon he joined the Giants in their second year in the NFL. There followed four years of All-League player honors and then the coaching job, for which he's never had a contract—indicating the esteem in which he's held by the club-owning Mara family.

Since 1933, his Giants have won the Eastern Division crown eight times and the National League championship twice. Noted for his A-formation offense and stonewall defenses, it's a tribute to Owen's ability that a player as great as Don Hutson scored only four of his 100 NFL touchdowns against the Giants and "Slingin' Sammy" Baugh tossed an average of only one touchdown in every 30 passes against the New Yorkers.

The Giants won their first league title in 1927, with Owen tackle and captain. He's gone a long way in football since—quite a trip for a fellow who rode to his first game on a cowpony.

KENNETH (KEN) STRONG
(*New York University, '29*)
STAPLETON, 1929-1932.
NEW YORK GIANTS, 1933-35.
NEW YORK YANKEES, 1936-1937.
NEW YORK GIANTS, 1939.
JERSEY CITY GIANTS, 1940.
NEW YORK GIANTS, 1943-   .

One of the truly great football players of our time, and perhaps anybody's time, is Ken Strong. Whenever all-time All-America discussions come up you'll always hear Strong's name mentioned with fellows like Nagurski, Thorpe, Nevers, Grange, etc.

As a college star, Ken gained unanimous All-America honors in 1928. He led the nation in scoring with 153 points and 21 touchdowns. He kicked 27 extra points, a skill which in 1946 enabled him to create an all-time scoring record in New York Giants' history.

He was a great punter and blocking back. In his senior year, Strong was switched to tailback and became the nation's offensive star, gaining an unbelievable total of 2200 yards rushing. And while he was no Baugh or Luckman, his passing was adequate.

Ken carried his ability into the pro ranks and became an immediate success. In 1934, he was All-League halfback, following a freshman season in which he tied for the scoring leadership. The giants never were to be sorry they wangled him from Stapleton, with whom Strong started his pro career (1929-32).

After the 1935 campaign, Strong jumped the NFL to play with the New York Yankees in an outlaw league. For his two years in the unrecognized circuit, he was banned from playing in the National League until the Giants re-signed him in 1939.

Strong hooked up with the Jersey City Giants in 1940 and came back to the parent club in 1943. In 1944, more than a decade after making his pro debut, Ken's educated toe produced six field goals to add another title to his string.

On November 24, 1946, in the Polo Grounds, thousands of fans paid belated tribute to a great athlete on "Ken Strong Day."

He put the "kick" in the New York Giants—Ken Strong.

STEVE OWEN AND KEN STRONG
New York Giants 30, Chicago Bears 13.
NATIONAL LEAGUE CHAMPIONSHIP, NEW YORK, DECEMBER 9, 1934.

(Editor's Note: Steve Owen and Ken Strong each selected the famous "Basketball Shoes Game," in which the Giants won the 1934 NFL crown, as his "Greatest Day in Football."

Owen, looking at it from the coach's angle, relates the thrilling story in which his Giants scored 27 points in the fourth period on a frozen field, in zero weather. Strong, the star of the game, says simply: "I scored two touchdowns, a field goal and two extra points for a total of 17 points.")

The National Football League records show that the New York Giants defeated the Chicago Bears, 30 to 13, for the championship on December 8, 1934. The score, of course, doesn't tell the story at all. The Giants won, true. But how they won is another tale and one of the most dramatic football has ever witnessed.

This game was supposed to be a cinch for the Chicago Bears. They were terrific. They possessed a 31-game unbeaten streak that stretched way back to November of 1933 when Ken Strong, then a freshman Giant, booted a field goal to beat them, 3 to 0. We, the Giants, were weak by comparison. We had squeezed through to the Eastern Division crown with a record of eight won and five lost.

They had Bronko Nagurski, who was still ripping defensives asunder like paper bags; the brilliant Keith Molesworth; a raging pair of ends in Bill Karr and Bill Hewitt and ferocious linemen like George Musso and Link Lyman. We, on the other hand, had a handful of veterans like Ray Flaherty, Dale Burnett, Bo Molenda, Bill Morgan and a couple of newcomer hopefuls in Mel Hein, Ed Danowski and Strong.

As though I didn't have enough to worry about the morning of the game, the telephone rang in my room and I received a gloomy message from Jack Mara, then treasurer of the club. He was calling from the Polo Grounds and wanted me to know that the field was frozen. I shivered . . . or maybe, quivered. Anyway, we were in a tough spot, because it would be impossible to run on a field that was so hard that football cleats would slide as though it was ice.

It was Flaherty, the captain of the team, who came to me and suggested we wear sneakers. Flaherty had worn a pair in a 1925 game that his Gonzaga team played with Montana. They had also been used in 1933 by the University of Washington against the Seattle All-Stars, helping the Huskies roll up a 69-0 halftime score. Washington, congenially, loaned the Stars sneakers for the scoreless second half.

Flaherty's idea turned the trick and, ironically, made a hero out of Strong. I say "ironically" because those two, when Ken played with rival Stapleton, had been keen rivals. They had been in many grudge battles. One time, for instance, Ray grabbed a pass in Strong's territory and ran for a touchdown. Standing in the end zone, Flaherty thumbed his nose at Ken and ridiculed: "The great, All-America Strong."

At another time, we were playing on the Stapleton field in Staten Island, which was pretty small and had a fence almost smack up against the sidelines. Strong headed around Flaherty's end and Ray got a headlock on him and dragged Ken down near the white stripe.

In those days, you were forced to put the ball in play where it was downed, not like today where they move the ball away from the sidelines towards the middle of the field. Well, Strong was trying to wriggle out-of-bounds and Flaherty's headlock was getting tighter and tighter. Finally, the officials had to pull Ray off Ken, who was almost choking to death.

When they separated the players, Flaherty still felt thuds on his helmet that he thought had been coming from Strong's fists. Ray turned around and, there, leaning over the fence, was a little old lady rapping him with her umbrella.

Getting back to the basketball shoes, however. Flaherty solved our problem with his idea. Now, all we had to do was get the sneakers. Thus, on short notice, we began our hunt. By the time they were dug up, out of Manhattan College's supply, and arrived at the Polo Grounds, the game had started. We played the first half in regulation regalia and in weather so cold that many of the 37,000 fans wore overshoes, boots or heavy woolen stockings over their regular shoes to keep their feet from freezing.

There was no stopping the mighty Bears in the first half with the great Nagurski raging along with complete disdain for the slippery footing. Strong put us in front with a 38-yard field goal in the first quarter and that was all we got in the half. Nagurski started bulling his way down the field and powered over for a second quarter score. A little later, Jack Manders booted a 17-yard field goal and we trailed, 10 to 3, at intermission.

We put on our basketball shoes in the locker room at halftime and came out hoping it would help us overcome the big deficit. It didn't look too good at the start of the third period, because Manders again kicked a field goal, this time from 23 yards out, and we trailed, 13 to 3.

As we entered the fourth quarter, there seemed little doubt in the minds of almost everyone—even mine, to tell the truth—that we could overcome the Bears. Strong, our best runner, had injured his leg shortly before the end of the first half when Lyman hit him a vicious tackle. Besides that, Ken's feet were so cold in the basketball shoes—which he was wearing for the first time in a football game—that they were numb and immune to pain; immune to the normal pain of punting in a soft shoe and an injured toenail besides.

It was Danowski and Ike Frankian who put us back in the game. Fordham Ed passed us down field until we reached scoring distance. Then Danowski flipped into the end zone, with Frankian making an unbelievable catch for the touchdown. Brumbaugh seemed to have intercepted the pass but whether he and Frankian caught it at the same time or Ike wrested it from his hands, nobody will know. Anyway, we had a score and Strong's kick made it 13 to 10.

Our guys were really hopped up; flitting and darting on the frozen field in their sneakers like sure-footed matadors while the burly Bears were sliding around like raging Bulls. We forced and drove the Bears all over the place; forced them into a break which turned out to be the winning touchdown. Hurried on a punt, Molesworth kicked out only 25 yards to his 48 and Strong brought it back seven.

With the aid of Lou Little, the Columbia coach who'd been spotting Bear weaknesses from the stands and phoning me on the bench, we went to town. From the 41, Strong followed Molenda and Danowski through a gaping hole at tackle opened by Morgan. Off to the races went Ken, almost hitting an official and then flashing into the open. Brumbaugh and Sisk tried to stop him, but Strong's speed was too great in sneakered feet that prevented him from slipping. He scored as the crowd poured out on the field, yelling, dancing, half-hysterical with excitement.

Strong added the extra point and it was 17 to 13 favoring the Giants. That wasn't the end. The mighty Bears, dazed and disappointed, yielded two more touchdowns before bowing to an underdog that didn't believe in records or reputations. Strong and Danowski got the last two scores, but they were only for the record books. The game was over when Strong stepped sure-footedly on his 41-yard touchdown run.

We used only four subs that game—Jack McBride, who faced the Bears for the 19th time; the late Len Grant; Kink Richards and my brother Bill. We didn't need any more. All we needed were the basketball shoes. Thank goodness they arrived on time.

Nagurski said it when he declared: "I think the sneakers gave them an edge in the last half. They were able to cut back when they were running with the ball and we couldn't cut with them."

It was a great victory, one in which every man on the team chipped in his bit. Danowski's passing, Strong's punting and running and the terrific line play of Morgan. That—and the sneakers—is what did it.

Morgan, the defensive hero of the game who did a great job of stopping Nagurski, was showered with questions after it was over. His modest answer:

"My hardest assignment was getting through the crowd into the dressing room."

The lineup:
CHICAGO

(13)	pos.	NEW YORK (30)
Hewitt	le	Frankian
Lyman	lt	Morgan
Pearson	lg	Gibson
Kawal	c	Hein
Carlson	rg	Jones
Musso	rt	Irvin
Karr	re	Flaherty
Brumbaugh	qb	Danowski
Ronzani	lh	Burnett
Molesworth	rh	Strong
Nagurski	fb	Molenda

Chicago .... 0—10—3—0——13
New York .... 3—0—0—27——30

Touchdowns: *New York*—Strong, 2, Danowski. *Chicago*—Frankian, Nagurski.

Points after touchdowns: *New York*—Strong, 2. *Chicago*—Molenda, Manders.

Field goals: *Chicago*—Manders, 2. *New York*—Strong.

Substitutions: *Giants*—McBride, Richards, Owen, Grant. *Bears*—Manders, Johnsos, Buss, Sisk, Rosequist, Miller, Masterson.

Referee—Bob Cahn, Illinois. Umpire—Bull Lowe, Dartmouth. Field Judge—Judge Meyer, Ohio Wesleyan. Linesman—George Vergara, Notre Dame.

RAYMOND W. (DUCKY) POND

(*Yale, '25*)

YALE, 1925.

THE HOTCHKISS SCHOOL, 1926-1927.

YALE, 1928.

YALE SCRUBS, 1929-1933.

YALE VARSITY, 1934-1940.

BATES COLLEGE, 1945-   .

Among the leading names in the poll for the 1946 Coach of the Year, was Raymond W. (Ducky) Pond, of Bates College, Lewiston, Maine. It seemed strange to see Ducky Pond anywhere except at his beloved Yale, but the ruddy-faced, blue-eyed native of Torrington, Conn., had lost none of his magic touch with athletic youth—leading Bates to an undefeated regular season and national recognition.

Ducky Pond was a better than average halfback on Yale's last undefeated and untied team—the 1923 eleven coached by the immortal Tad Jones. He ran 70 yards to a touchdown against Harvard in 1923 and dashed 48 to a score against Army the following year. The great Walter Camp, dean of football authorities, thought enough of his ability to name him on the second All-America team of 1924.

A sound football fundamentalist, Pond proved he has the supreme gift of leadership. No better example of that came in 1934, when he took over as head coach of Yale's meager football fortunes. Along with his master strategist, Greasy Neale, he rebuilt a team weak in number and reserve as well as experience and tuned it to a pitch that produced one of the greatest upsets of all-time—the 7-0 victory on November 17th which ended the 17-game winning streak of Fritz Crisler's mighty Princeton machine.

Pond has a way of instilling spirit into a group. He makes decisions, sticks with them and, has no false pride of using another coach's plays if it will help his team.

Possibly the finest tribute to his ability as leader and as coach came from Neale, a man who could have had at the time any number of head-coaching jobs of his own. Asked whether he intended to return to Yale, Neale replied:

"You bet I will if Ducky wants me. He's a wonderful chap to work for."

Three years in the service, between 1941 and 1944, did not dull any of Pond's coaching skill.

DUCKY POND
Yale 7, Princeton 0.
PRINCETON, NOVEMBER 17, 1934.

My greatest day in football?

Beating Princeton anytime is a great day in any Blue's life. You can imagine the way I felt this particular day—approaching the windup of my first year as head coach of Yale football, and finishing with a victory over a powerful Princeton team that had rolled up 17 straight victories and hadn't been beaten since Michigan's 14-7 triumph in 1932.

To make this day even more unforgettable, we played 11 men 60 minutes against Fritz Crisler's Tigers, who had crushed six previous opponents, rolled up 242 points and yielded a mere 18. But November 17th, 1934, was Yale's day—a day we had been pointing for. The team lived up to my expectations. It had to face a great test against a great rival and it won in magnificent fashion.

There undoubtedly have been greater heroes in Yale football history than these eleven men but I know that what they accomplished on that New Brunswick gridiron that afternoon will find a permanent niche in Eli football annals. Bob "Choo-Choo" Train, Meredith Scott, Clare Curtin, Jimmy DeAngelis, Paul Grosscup, Henry Wright, Larry Kelley, Jerry Roscoe, Stan Fuller, Stratford Merton and Matt Whitehead—they were Yale's eleven strong men. They were keyed for this battle—carefully groomed from the first day of the season under the patient, brilliant tutoring of such experts as Greasy Neale, Ivan Williamson and Denny Myers. True, we had lost close games to Columbia, Army and Georgia, but the boys were ready and inspired for the rampaging, heavily favored Tigers.

It was Bob Zuppke, of Illinois, who once said:

"Give me one game to win but tell me in advance which one it is and I'll win it."

That's what we did—that was our game to win.

Kelley, the master receiver, an All-America end on anybody's team, scored the winning touchdown on a pass from Roscoe in the first period but all eleven men earned this victory—they wrote their names high in the history of Yale athletics. Scoring against a team is

*Coach (Ducky) Pond and All-America end Larry Kelley at Yale,
1936.*

one thing, holding the opposition scoreless is another—and we succeeded in both departments. Princeton, for the first time that season, came against a line that carried the fight to it. Our fast-charging linemen made the "break" for the only score of the game.

Ken Sandbach juggled a kick by Curtin in the end zone and the Blue line was on him just as he got back on the field. The Tigers had to kick out and we had possession of the ball well in Nassau territory.

Gil Lea threw Morton for a loss on one play and we were back on the Princeton 43. The next play was from kick formation, with Fuller set to boot, but DeAngelis' wayward pass from center was short—Roscoe got it—and here the boys came through with some of the drilling they'd been getting all season. This was a tough spot, because the short pass from center was not premeditated.

Roscoe ran a few steps toward left end, turned and whipped a pass over left tackle to Kelley, waiting on Princeton's 29-yard line. Big Larry grabbed the ball and his run with it is one of the most remarkable I have ever witnessed. With an uncanny judgment of pace, he headed for the goal line, face to the sidelines. Without changing stride, he cut down toward the goal from 15 yards in. One black-shirted figure moved in on him but fell just short on the 23-yard line. Straight for the corner ran Kelley and, as he did, the Yale stands urged him on with a terrific roar.

Just inside the five-yard line, two of Princeton's fastest, Sandbach and Gary Levan, had Kelley cornered—and here for the first time, Kelley broke stride. He seemed to halt momentarily, then, starting again, virtually twisted and danced between the two bewildered Tigers like a ghost. Kelley scored standing and Curtin made it 7 to 0 with a perfect placement.

Keeping that lead against an enraged Tiger team was a Herculean task. Throughout the rest of the game, while the crowd waited for an outbreak of Princeton's vaunted power, the Yale defenses held.

In the second period, the Tigers had first down inside our five-yard stripe but, miraculously, we held for downs on the one. On another occasion, they reached our nine, but they were forever being rushed by our forward wall. Their passes were hurried, inaccurate—Princeton completed only two of 14 attempts.

It was a great victory, well deserved, for eleven men who, for one day, at least, reached an unbelievable peak. This was no ordinary team and Princeton played a great game, too. Lea was a fine end, Levan a daring runner and brilliant defensive back, and Captain Mose Kalbough a superb center throughout. Yale was never safe until the final gun. The Tigers had outrushed us by almost 100 yards but our passing and punting, protected and backed by an unyielding, hard-charging line, turned the trick.

It is appropriate here to tell of Kelley's amazing ability not only to catch passes but to talk things up on the field. His was a flaming spirit that instilled the others with that same will to win. After Princeton's early fumbles, Kelley said to quarterback Kadlic:

"Say, Kadlic, has the Rose Bowl got handles on it?"

It seems that Princeton students had circulated a petition on the Nassau campus to send the Tigers to Pasadena. But that was before the Yale game.

On another occasion, when a Tiger sub could find no halfback willing to be replaced late in the game, Kelley spoke up:

"Hey, Mr. Referee, maybe that substitute is for me. I've been playing in the Princeton backfield all afternoon."

Only the name of Kelley can be found in the list of All-Time Yale greats—for Old Eli, through the thrill-steeped years, had produced some of the mightiest football heroes of the game—but Yale will never forget those Iron Men of 1934. Roscoe was a much better passer than he was ever given credit for being, but Kelley on the receiving end made it look too easy for any one throwing the ball. I was fortunate, two years later—1936—to have another great quarterback throwing to Kelley, a fellow by the name of Clint Frank. They, too, beat Princeton in a game some consider the most spectacular of the long series.

This was one of those seasaw battles, one that ended 26 to 23, in Yale's favor. Yale led, 20 to 16, following a 26-yard pass from Frank to Kelley, who ran another 20 yards for the score. But Princeton tallied again and, with the game nearing a finish, that 23-20 lead looked big. Bottled on his own goal line, Frank threw a desperation, wobbly pass far up to midfield. Nobody seemed near it but almost out of nowhere appeared Kelley and his long arm and magnetic fingers gathered the ball in despite the presence of Tiger players around him. That set up the winning touchdown.

The thrill of that game, too, is something I'll remember, but nobody will ever take away from me my greatest of days—the day that Yale turned back a hitherto undaunted and unconquered Tiger for what to this day is considered among the most stunning upsets in football history.

The lineup:

YALE (7)	pos.	PRINCETON (0)
Train	le	Delaney
Scott	lt	Stoess
Curtin	lg	Weller
DeAngelis	c	Kalbough
Grosscup	rg	John
Wright	rt	Chamberlain
Kelley	re	Lea
Roscoe	qb	Kadlic
Fuller	rh	Sandbach
Morton	lh	Levan
Whitehead	fb	Constable
Yale	7—0—0—0——7	
Princeton	0—0—0—0——0	

Touchdown: *Yale*—Kelley.

Point after touchdown: *Yale*—Curtin.

Substitutions: *Yale*—none. *Princeton*—MacMillan, Montgomery, Spofford, Maufman, Pauk, Ritter, Kopf, Rulon-Miller.

Referee—W. T. Halloran, Providence. Umpire—T. J. Thorp, Columbia. Field Judge—J. E. Keegan, Pittsburgh. Linesman— L. A. Young, Pennsylvania.

KNUTE K. ROCKNE
(*Notre Dame, '14*)

There is no way to measure the comparative greatness of foot-ball players or coaches but regardless of what system is used the name of Knute Rockne will be right at the top.

No period in Notre Dame football history has been as great, nor as steeped with drama than that between 1911 and 1930, when the Rock reigned as player and coach. His contributions to the national football scene, too, are mighty and many, and along with such names as Alonzo Stagg, Pop Warner, Walter Camp, Gil Dobie, Bob Zuppke and "Hurry Up" Yost he has gone down in the records not only as a pioneer and builder of football teams but of men as well.

End on the Notre Dame teams of 1911, 1912 and 1913, and cap-tain of the 1913 team which was undefeated and untied and startled the country with its amazing use of the forward pass. Gus Dorais to Knute Rockne was as famous a pass-combination as you'll see in the record books.

The Rock took over the head coaching job for the Ramblers in 1918 and right there began a parade of great teams and great players. They still talk of George (The Gipper) Gipp, the Four Horsemen and the Seven Mules and more All-Americas than any other team can boast. From the fifth game of 1918 to the ninth game of 1921, Notre Dame was unbeaten on the gridiron, a total of 40 games in which the Irish scored 1097 points and gave up only 151. There were undefeated seasons on five occasions, including the last two teams he ever coached—1929 and 1930 which many consider his finest elevens. He was the first to use "shock troops" in football, and introduced the "Notre Dame shift."

Rockne's untimely death in an airplane accident in March, 1931, was a severe blow to the entire world. He was more than a coach. He was a scholar, a wit, and gifted too with an unusual kindness and devotion to his players. They'll never forget The Rock. No less than 89 of his players went forth to coach and to immortalize further the Rockne glory.

KNUTE ROCKNE'S GREATEST DAYS

(By Walter Kennedy)

To pick Knute Rockne's greatest day in football would be like picking the best of the Eight Wonders of the World. No one with whom I have spoken, among Notre Dame's football players and students and athletic officials of the Rockne era, remembers Rock ever singling out his favorite day or game. Therefore we can only guess.

It might have been the day of the first meeting between Notre Dame and Army, in 1913, when Rockne was captain and end of a team that was labelled as coming from South Bend, "Illinois." Notre Dame was an unknown quantity in those days and few, if any, ever heard of South Bend outside of the State of Indiana. The boys set out to erase the slur to the Hoosier State and also to surprise an Army team that was scheduled to walk right over the Irish.

With little Gus Dorais on the passing end, big Eichenlaub, fullback, providing the power, and Rockne and Pliska doing the catching, Notre Dame made history that day by swamping Army, 35 to 13. It was the first demonstration of the use of air power to overcome land power and it set the pace for the skillful and deceptive use of the pass. Rockne scored once, Eichenlaub twice and Pliska twice in that ball game.

Then again it might have been the Army-Notre Dame game of 1920, when the great George "The Gipper" Gipp staged an astound-

Rockne of Notre Dame.

ing one-man demonstration in the second half to whip Army, 27 to 17. His brief association with the Gipper must have been a pleasant, dramatic chapter in his book of life. To him, Gipp was the greatest all-around football player he ever coached.

There was the day that Rockne played against Jim Thorpe and his Carlisle Indians. He told that story to us on more than one occasion even though the joke was on him.

"In the review of my playing career," he narrated, "one hard day stands out above all others—the day I tried to stop the greatest football player of all, the Indian Jim Thorpe.

"My job was to tackle Thorpe, which I did successfully and with much suffering three times. After the third time Thorpe smiled genially at me.

" 'Be a good boy,' he said, 'Let Jim run.' "

"He took the ball again and I went at him. Never before have I received such a shock. It was as if a locomotive had hit me and been followed by a ten-ton truck rambling over the remains. I lay on the field of battle while Thorpe pounded out a 40-yard run for a touchdown.

"He came back, helped me to my feet, patted me fraternally on the back and, smiling broadly, said:

" 'That's a good boy, Knute. You let Jim run.' "

Rockne's pep talks between halves are famous and they must have provided him with a great many thrilling days. No other coach could inspire a team like the Rock did, and there was a versatility in his speeches all backed by sound psychology and knowledge of the men he coached.

In a game against a powerful Western Conference opponent, the Ramblers didn't do so well in the first half. They made countless errors and Rockne was thoroughly disgusted. The players went back to the dressing room dejected and awaiting not too anxiously the wrath of Rockne. The rest period ticked away and Rockne didn't show up. The players sat silent, bewildered until 30 seconds before the start of the second half. Just then, Rockne stuck his head in the door. The players jumped up, not knowing what to expect. And Rockne snapped:

"Okay, half a minute left. Let's go, GIRLS!"

Notre Dame was a fighting fury in that second half and won the game in a breeze.

Knute Rockne, Notre Dame; Tad Jones, Yale and Pop Warner, Stanford selecting 1927 All-Americas.

Rock is known as a football strategist and a molder of character and a maker of champions. He was all of that. He could fire up a team, with his withering blasts and his sarcasm and his jibes, like no one else before or since. Many players, who played under Rock, say he won games for them in the dressing room, when he charged them up to play better than they knew how.

It was on November 10, 1928, that Rock delivered his finest performance, and perhaps this was the game he would select above all others for his all time favorite—his greatest day in football. It was the day that a comparatively poor Notre Dame team met a great Army team. The Irish that year had already lost twice, and had won three games by one—touchdown spreads, against opponents like Loyola of New Orleans, Navy and Penn State. Everything pointed to a Kaydet win, and when the first half at the Yankee Stadium finished in a scoreless tie, it only served to heighten the interest in a second-half slaughter of the boys from South Bend.

Rock was very quiet that day, as the tired Irish licked their bruises and rested their weary bodies between halves. The veterans on the team waited for Rock's usual bombastic "fight" talk to start. Then, with a couple of minutes to go before the team had to return to the field, Rockne shooed out the few dressing room visitors and began the simplest, most dramatic talk of his career.

"Eight years ago," he said, "a young man was dying in South Bend. We were pretty close and I was at his bedside to see whether there was anything I could do. As I left the room to go, that boy called me back and whispered:

"'Some time, Rock, when the team is up against it and the breaks are going against the boys and things are wrong, tell them to go in and win one for the Gipper. I don't know where I'll be then, Rock, but I'll know about it and I'll be happy.'"

"This is the game, boys! This is the one I think that George Gipp would want us to win. Let's go!!"

After Army drove to a touchdown midway in the third period, the Irish came back 80 yards to score. It was then that the late Jack Chevigny uttered his immortal phrase, even as he was plunging across for the touchdown:

"There's one for the Gipper."

Later, in the fourth period, "One Play" Johnny O'Brien grabbed a pass from Johnny Niemec to win the game and Notre Dame had come up with one of the game's greatest upsets . . . inspired, even the boys themselves said, by what has always been called Rockne's greatest pep talk.

The lineup:

NOTRE DAME

(12)	pos.	ARMY (6)
E. Collins	le	Carlmark
Towmey	lt	Sprague
Law	lg	Hammack
Moynihan	c	Hall
Leppig	rg	Humber
Miller	rt	Perry
Vezle	re	Messinger
Brady	qb	Nave
Chevigny	lh	O'Keefe
Niemec	rh	Cagle
F. Collins	fb	Murrell
Notre Dame		0—0—6—6——12
Army		0—0—6—0——6

Touchdowns: *Army*—Murrell. *Notre Dame*—Chevigny, O'Brien.

Substitutions: *Notre Dame*—Colrick, Cannon, Carideo, Dew, O'Brien. *Army*—Allan, Dibb, Parham, Lynch, Maxwell, Walsh, Gibner, Piper, Hutchinson.

Referee—Walter Eckersall, Chicago. Umpire—Tom Thorp, Columbia. Field Judge—N. E. Kearns, DePaul. Head Linesman —F. W. Murphy, Brown.

Knute Rockne, football's greatest coach, gives his team a pep talk shortly before his untimely death.

AMOS ALONZO STAGG
(*Yale, '89*)
SPRINGFIELD COLLEGE, 1890-1891.
UNIVERSITY OF CHICAGO, 1892-1932.
COLLEGE OF THE PACIFIC, 1933-1946.
SUSQUEHANNA COLLEGE, 1947- .

"No man ever took into sport more lofty ideals or ever carved out for himself a more honorable career than the millions of his friends claim for 'Lon' Stagg."

No truer words were ever spoken about a man who, after 58 consecutive years of coaching declares simply:

"I'm too young to retire."

Stagg is considered football's greatest inventor as well as "The Grand Old Man of Football," and its symbol for character and sportsmanship. He has contributed, among countless other plays and formations, such famous offenses and defenses as ends back—halfbacks on defensive line—turtle back—fake kickoff—double delayed pass— double pass with forward pass—sliding offensive end. In 1889, he invented the tackling dummy.

The man who in his years of activity has seen and coached the greatest has never made an "All" selection.

"Although," he says, "I was selected as end on the first All-America team, I have steadfastly refused to select All-America, All-Western and All-Conference teams."

His selection as Coach of the Year in 1943, at the age of 81, is probably one of the most dramatic and nostalgic moments of sports. He richly deserved the honor—this mighty coaching immortal of the perennially bare head and snow-white hair. His way of rebuking a player was to call him "jackass" and there are many, including some of the truly greats, who are proud to be members of "Lon" Stagg's "Jackass Club."

AMOS ALONZO STAGG

My "greatest day in football" is every day of my more than 62 years of playing and coaching. As I wrote Chancellor Tully C. Knoles, of the College of the Pacific, "Consistency of living had been my prayer. I am fully convinced that the pearl of great price to me is to continue my life's purpose of helping young men through the relationship of coaching."

That was the reason that I did not accept the proposal to remain at the University of Chicago at a large salary . . . that is the reason why I moved on to Susquehanna from the College of the Pacific.

I have had great days which thrilled me and left an indelible stamp on my mind. One was the day when President William Rainey Harper, of the new University of Chicago, asked me to become the director of the pioneer Department of Physical Culture and Athletics, a day which went on to become 41 years of happy relationship. From then on the great days piled on.

Possibly one of my outstanding memories is coaching Walter Eckersall. His skill, tenacity, speed and headwork made this man a marvel. He weighed 143 pounds and yet was tireless. He twice kicked five field goals in a game—against Illinois in 1905, and Nebraska in 1906. In 1903, he beat Wisconsin almost single-handed with three field goals, and the papers shouted "Eckersall 15, Wisconsin 6." (Ed. note—the field goal counted five points then.)

They called my 1905 team a football masterpiece. That was my first undefeated and untied season—we scored 245 points and gave

Football was the topic when Amos Alonzo Stagg and Fielding
(Hurry-up) Yost meet in 1931.

away five, to Indiana, in 10 games. That was the team of Eckersall,
Leo Detray, Fred Hitchcock, Ed Parry, Bubbles Hill, Babe Meigh,
Burt Gale, Russell, Art Badenoch, Walker, Hugo Bezdek and Captain Mark Catlin—a team that moved on quietly but relentlessly to
the day it met mighty Michigan for the Western Conference championship. Michigan, under "Hurry Up" Yost, seemed invincible.
The Wolverines "Point-a-Minute-Men" had roared through five
seasons of victory—only one tie in 56 games marred this amazing
record and only 40 points had been scored against them. The immortal Willie Heston had moved on from Michigan at the end of
the 1904 season but they had names like "Germany" Schulz, "Indian" Schulte, Johnny Garrels, "Octy" Graham, Fred Norcross,
Shorty Longman, Tom and Harry Hammond, and Captain Joe
Curtis.

   There were more than 25,000 in Marshall Field on the Midway
that Thanksgiving Day in 1905—the greatest crowd in the history of
Western football—and I doubt if too many gave the Maroons much

of a chance. This was one game I wanted to win. The previous Spring, as track coach, Michigan's Keene Fitzpatrick and I had gone through two trivial disputes, Keene wanted to change the order of events which had been agreed on in the contract. Yost had tried to intercede once, and naturally I objected. Yost's parting remark was: "I'll give you plenty next Fall."

In the dressing room before the game, I told the boys the story, adding:

"Boys, I don't want this game stuffed down my throat."

It was a turning point in Western Conference history. We won it, 2 to 0, on a play that illustrates fully the ferocity with which the game was fought. It started out and was most of the way a punting duel between Eckersall and Garrels. The "break" came when Eckersall kicked over the Michigan goal line. He had set the play up in a preliminary way by running out from behind his own goal line to our 22-yard line from kick formation, illustrating once again his astounding ability to think quickly. The over-the-goal punt followed shortly afterward. Denny Clark, substitute halfback for Michigan, scooped up the ball and started off to the left.

As Chicago runners rushed down on him, Clark crossed the goal line diagonally but just after he stepped onto the playing field, Art Badenoch, Maroon right tackle, tackled him low and Captain Mark Catlin, right end, dashed in and caught him high and pushed him behind the goal line for a safety. That meant the ball game that has gone into history as one of the most famous of all time. For years, Clark was blamed for his "failure" and the criticism and ridicule was erroneously said to have affected his later life.

Chicago ended Michigan's five-year reign with that triumph. In 1908 Michigan withdrew from the Western Conference not to return until 1917.

We had another unbeaten and untied season at Chicago in 1913—the only other in my career as a coach—and I can still recall with a sense of satisfaction how those Maroons went through the season. They were generally a kidding, horseplaying crew but in one important game they were quite different. That was against Purdue, and the score of that one read Chicago 6, Purdue 0.

Purdue had not beaten Chicago in 15 years, but they had a great team that season and the newspapers headlined my respect for them. "Stagg Fears Purdue," they cried.

Andy Smith was coach of the Boilermakers, and he had the mighty Elmer Oliphant striding at his best. He had Applegate, O'Brien and Finn in the backfield with Oliphant, and two great line blockers in Glossup and Usher. The week before Purdue had tied Wisconsin, 1912 champions, 7 to 7.

Perhaps ours was a team of destiny. At tackles we had Goettler, who went on to win the Medal of Honor in bringing food to the Lost Battalion, and Shull, who was given the Distinguished Service Cross. Both were killed in France. Baumgartner, Huntington and Vruwink were our ends, and Harris and Scanlon, guards. The great Des Jardien was at center, and our backfield was composed of Pierce, Gray, Norgren and Pete Russell.

The teams were equally matched in physical ability. The game was hard-fought and fierce all the way. On one occasion, Norgren, on the second All-America the year before, unleashed such a hard flying tackle that Oliphant did a complete cartwheel in the air, landing on his feet but facing the wrong way. Elmer ran ten yards toward his own goal before realizing it. Pete Russell, now president of the Harris Trust and Savings Bank in Chicago, drop-kicked two field goals for our margin of victory.

Defeat sometimes stands out in your mind as much as victory and well do I remember how Princeton beat one of my strongest elevens in 1922. In 1921, the Maroon fullbacks were a physically powerful trio, so much so that it had the enemy chanting:

"Timme, Thomas and Zorn,
 We wish they'd never been born."

These were the fullbacks of a team that didn't win any prizes but was one of the most feared in the country. Our 1922 eleven lost Timme but had gained some strength elsewhere.

We played Princeton after three successive victories to pave the way. The Tigers, coached by the late Bill Roper, were not given much of a chance to beat us. Chicago had captured the first game of the series in 1921, 9 to 0, and they were supposed to be weaker and Chicago stronger.

Going into the fourth period, Chicago was ahead, 18 to 7, and it looked like certain victory for us. Cagey Bill Roper, however, with nothing to lose, virtually demoralized the Maroons by passing instead of kicking from his two-yard line. The tide turned with that. Before Chicago realized it, the score was 18 to 14, and a final drive, aided by interference and an offside penalty, made it 21 for Princeton and 18 for Chicago.

With only two minutes left, the Maroons ran wild. Pass after pass brought the ball to Princeton's one-yard line but there an inspired Tiger eleven held to win the ball game.

There was also the battle in 1924 against Red Grange and Illinois. I won my last Big Ten Conference championship that year and we got a tremendous thrill tying Illinois, 21 to 21. We made only one mistake that game—letting Grange get the ball three times—the same Galloping Ghost who had scored five touchdowns against Michigan, four coming in 12 minutes of play.

From Chicago, I moved to the College of the Pacific and my 14 years there hold memories that will never be erased. It gave me a chance to continue to teach what I knew best and you can imagine how I felt in 1943 when they named me Coach of the Year. For the first time this little college in Stockton, California, was considered in the National rating and our questionable defeat—by Southern California, 6 to 0, before 67,000 fans in the Coliseum at Los Angeles —was a heartbreaking event. I have steadfastly refused to select All-America, All-Western and All-Conference teams but were I doing that, Johnny Podesto, College of the Pacific tailback, would have received strong consideration.

Great days—yes—there were many and more to come, both in victory and defeat.

HARRY A. STUHLDREHER
(Notre Dame, '25)
HARTFORD BLUES, 1925.
BROOKLYN HORSEMEN, 1926.
VILLANOVA COLLEGE, 1925-1935.
WISCONSIN, 1936-   .

The *"Four Horsemen"* and the *"Seven Mules"* of Notre Dame are legendary figures in the annals of football—and Harry Stuhldreher was the mastermind. *"The Little General"* as they called him was Knute Rockne's only All-America contribution on the great 1924 team which won ten in an undefeated, untied season, and went on to crush Ernie Nevers and a mighty Stanford eleven in the Rose Bowl, 27 to 10.

A molder of character as well as of football players, Stuhldreher has developed some excellent teams and players in his more than 20 years of coaching. The University of Wisconsin was known as a football graveyard when he took over in 1936—and the Badgers came to life.

Stuhldreher has never won a Big Ten championship with the Badgers but they've come close more than once and have scored many an upset. His 1942 team, which won eight, lost one and tied one, earned him the honor of Big Ten Coach of the Year. The Badgers finished second behind Ohio State in the battle for the Conference title and had the satisfaction of beating the Buckeyes in their game that year. They also finished third in the National ratings— highest ever achieved by any Wisconsin eleven.

As a player, all 145 pounds of him, Stuhldreher ranks as one of the finest quarterbacks in Notre Dame's glorious history. He was an excellent passer and, despite his lack of weight, a dangerous runner.

Keen of wit and steeped in football lore, Stuhldreher will go down in history as one of the greats of the game, both as a player and as an inspirational leader.

HARRY STUHLDREHER
Wisconsin 14, Purdue 13.
LAFAYETTE, INDIANA, OCTOBER 26, 1940.

It took a "hunch" to give me my greatest day in football but that is getting ahead of the story.

There was nothing exceptional about the meeting of Wisconsin and Purdue in 1940. Neither team was going anywhere in particular and, aside from the fact that this was a traditional game in a series dating back to 1892, it was nothing to get excited about except from a local point of view. There was the fact, however, that since my arrival at Wisconsin in 1936, we had been unable to beat Purdue for three successive seasons. I wanted to win that year to break the spell but the story is not that we won, but how we did it.

Purdue had a powerful team that year—powerful compared to our Badgers who had been able to win only one game the previous year. And for 52 minutes of the game in Ross-Ade Stadium, Purdue's superiority was marked in every department of play.

We fought them as best we could, battling so viciously that with three quarters gone it was still a scoreless contest. The torrid fight seemed over, for all intent and purposes, when Purdue rolled up two quick touchdowns in the last quarter. With eight minutes left to play, Purdue led, 13 to 0. It was only natural that Coach Mal Elward, who was a teammate of Rockne's on Notre Dame's 1913 team, and his charges, could sit back and relax, feeling that the game was in the bag.

Why shouldn't they feel confident. Hadn't they seemingly scored enough points to win as Johnny Galvin slipped over left tackle to climax a 60-yard march with a 24-yard touchdown run, and sub halfback, Paul Anderson, followed with a quick 63-yard dash for another score? And what if we did block John Petty's attempt for the extra point after the second score. Wasn't 13 points enough for a team that had outplayed us all the way and had the clock, which read eight minutes to go, also on its side?

But suddenly the Badgers came to life. Putting the ball in play on our 16, we smashed and powered our way 84 yards in six plays. Bobby Ray, a soph fullback who had replaced George Paskvan, and was to become the hero of one of the most dramatic victories ever scored, plunged over center from the one-yard line for the touchdown. Tackle Fred Gage then converted and we trailed, 13 to 7.

There is no explaining how a mediocre team for nine-tenths of a game can astoundingly become a championship machine. You've seen it happen before in all sports but the answer to what provides the missing spark has not yet been discovered. It just happens—and it happened to Wisconsin.

Purdue followers stirred following our first touchdown but the fleeing hands of the big clock reassured them. Deliberate offensive action, designed to waste the remaining time left to play, was taken by the Boilermakers. But Fate intervened in the form of having Purdue strategy backfire into the winning touchdown for us.

Purdue took the kickoff and used up three plays on the ground as the clock tore off the seconds as though it was jet-propelled. With fourth down coming up and only a few plays left, the Boilermakers decided to rush the ball instead of kicking. We stopped them cold on their 35 and took over with but three seconds remaining—time for just one play.

It was sound thinking that led Purdue to rush instead of kick. A kick might be blocked. What could we do with 35 yards to go and one play to make it. The chances were 100 to 1 or better that we couldn't make it. We took time out to deliberate the chances and plan the last play of the game. It had to be a pass, a fact so obvious when we came out of our huddle that the Purdue defense automatically spread out anticipating the play. But for a defense that was prepared, the Purdue stalwarts proved unprepared for what we threw.

Johnny Tennant took the pass from center and raced to his right. He stopped short and fired diagonally to the left where end Ray Kreick was standing surprisingly all alone. He took the ball on the 10 and galloped for the tying touchdown as the final gun sounded.

With the game actually over, that all-important extra point had to be kicked. To this day, I don't know why I selected Bobby Ray to kick that ball instead of Gage, who had succeeded with the first one. Call it a hunch—call it destiny. A stadium full of Purdue and Wisconsin rooters sat breathless in the stands—and I confess that I wasn't exactly calm—as Ray waited amazingly cool for the ball to be snapped. And then it was over—the extra point and the game. Ray did it and Wisconsin collected a seemingly miraculous 14-13 victory.

That's why, in spite of the fact that I had played some thrilling and exciting football under a fellow called Rockne, I have to rate that game and that day my greatest. All things considered, it would be hard to equal the drama that it produced.

The lineup:

WISCONSIN

(14)	pos.	PURDUE (13)
Phillips	le	Rankin
Thornally	lt	Neft
Gile	lg	Miller
Henry	c	Axton
Gage	rg	Melton
Tornow	rt	Timperman
Lorenz	re	McCaffry
Farris	qb	Kersey
Hoskins	lh	Carter
Miller	rh	Berto
Paskvan	fb	Petty
Wisconsin	0—0—0—14——14	
Purdue	0—0—0—13——13	

Touchdowns: *Wisconsin*—Ray (sub for Paskvan); Kreich (sub for Lorenz); *Purdue*—Galvin (sub for Carter); Anderson (sub for Berto).

Points after touchdowns: *Wisconsin*—Gage, Ray; *Purdue*—Petty.

Referee—Frank Birch, Earlham. Umpire—Anthony Haines, Yale. Field Judge—Dr. E. F. Cigrand, Northwestern. Linesman—W. D. Knight, Dartmouth.

FRANK W. THOMAS
(Notre Dame, '22)
GEORGIA, 1923-1924.
CHATTANOOGA, 1925-1928.
GEORGIA, 1929-1930.
ALABAMA, 1931-1946.

Back in 1923, a Notre Dame graduate, on the recommendation of Knute Rockne, packed his bags and headed for the University of Georgia and a backfield coaching job. The youngster, becoming the first Irish graduate to coach at a major Southern school, was Frank Thomas. Over the years he was to gain the reputation as the leading exponent of the Notre Dame system in the South. When Harry Mehre joined Thomas as a Georgia line coach in 1924, they introduced the system by which Rockne's great teams thrived so successfully.

Thomas and Mehre became the first to conduct Spring football practices at Georgia, something they had learned as 1921 teammates at South Bend. Thomas went on alone to Chattanooga as head coach and in four seasons his teams won 26, lost eight and tied two, while capturing the old Southern Intercollegiate Athletic Association championship the last three seasons. The 1927 Chattanooga eleven was undefeated.

A football, baseball and basketball star at Western State Normal College in 1917 and 1918 before he enrolled at Notre Dame, Thomas returned to Georgia in 1929 and three seasons later took over the head-coaching reigns at Alabama. Illness forced him to give up active coaching for the job of athletic director at the end of the 1946 campaign.

Alabama's record under Thomas is one of the best, if not the best, in college ranks. Succeeding Wallace Wade in January, 1931, he proceeded to roll up a record of 98 victories, 21 losses and seven ties while winning four Southeastern Conference championships. He sent three teams into the Rose Bowl and one each to the Sugar, Cotton and Orange Bowls. His Crimson Tide elevens were undefeated in 1934 and 1945.

Thomas will always be remembered as one of Knute Rockne's brightest pupils.

FRANK THOMAS
Alabama 29, Stanford 13.

ROSE BOWL, JANUARY 1, 1935.

They called it aerial sleight of hand, and perhaps it was, but the Crimson Tide team that I sent into the Rose Bowl against Stanford on January 1, 1935, was capable of almost anything.

A decided underdog despite the fact that we had gone through the season undefeated and untied, we took the field against Stanford's bonecrushing "Laughing Boys" and proved to the immense crowd of 85,000—the largest ever to see a Rose Bowl game up to that time—that the 1934 Crimson Tide eleven was a highly underrated aggregation.

Coming from behind, with Millard (Dixie) Howell and Don Hutson electrifying the crowd and the Stanford players with one of the greatest passing and running exhibitions I've ever seen, we beat the Indians, 29 to 13. I doubt if any day could be more memorable for me than the one that provided a comparatively young coach not only with his first undefeated season but with a victory in the Rose Bowl when it was the number one game of the nation.

It is not true that Alabama was an ordinary running team, even against the power that belonged to Stanford. In fact, our season's victories were scored chiefly on long runs. Against Stanford, except for one beautiful touchdown run by Howell, our ground game was somewhat off. But we had planned a passing game.

Frank W. Thomas, a big name in Alabama football history.

"Our only chance," I had told the boys prior to the game, "is through the air. We must stop their great forwards and power plays. I'm not sure that we can, but they'll be watching our runners so we'll do it by passing."

Stanford's coach, Claude (Tiny) Thornhill, was quoted as saying:

"It'll take a great team to beat Stanford."

Well, a great team did beat them—the greatest I ever coached.

We could do nothing against Stanford's powerful forward wall in the first period. Howell's booming punts saved us temporarily but a fumble gave Stanford the ball on our 27 late in the quarter. Joe Demyanovich dropped the ball when tackled and the alert Keith Topping recovered for the Indians. Paced by the big boy with the piston-like legs, Bobby Grayson, Stanford blasted away to the first touchdown. Grayson plunged over from the one and, when Monk Moscrip kicked the extra point, it was 7 to 0 against us. The 2500 Alabama supporters who had come all the way from home to cheer us from the big rose-decorated stand, had nothing to yell about. It seemed as if the expected rout was on.

Stanford's cheers were still ringing in our ears when the Crimson Tide began to put on the greatest display of forward passing seen in the 20-year history of the Rose Bowl. It may be that we had nothing to match the tremendous drive of Stanford but we showed the record-breaking throng something that left them gasping for breath when it was over. We tried only 13 passes but completed the amazing total of ten for 216 yards. There was enough action and drama in the second period alone to fill a dozen football games.

After Stanford's touchdown we never gave up the ball until we scored. Howell ran the kickoff back 24 yards to the 45 and passed to Hutson on Stanford's 27. Then Howell flipped to Jim Angelich to put the ball on the 16. We lost on a running play, but another pass, to Paul Bryant, brought us to the five and Howell dashed over from there. Riley Smith missed the kick and it was 7 to 6. But with the rapidity of a cyclone the score soon read Alabama 22, Stanford 7.

Stanford kicked over the goal line, Howell raced 19 yards and then heaved to Hutson on Stanford's 32. Two plays later, on a pass to Hutson, the ball was again on the Indians' five-yard line. The breaks were with us, too. Hutson fumbled when tackled but Bryant recovered. Several plays afterward, Smith dropped back to the 20 and calmly kicked a field goal from placement that put us ahead, 9 to 7.

Again Stanford kicked off and Howell brought it back to the 26-yard line. Angelich ran to the 33 and the versatile Howell produced the bombshell that further bewildered Stanford by breaking away on a 67-yard touchdown run. Not a Stanford man touched him. Moscrip, who played a brilliant game for the Indians, had the only chance to reach Howell but he slipped and the elusive Dixie raced by.

With only one minute to play in the first half, Smith intercepted a Stanford pass on its 46. Then Joe Riley passed to Hutson, who caught the ball on the 30 and ran the rest of the way to score. Hutson missed the extra point as the second period ended. It was a completely dazed Stanford team that left the field at half-time, trailing 22 to 7.

As far as the score went, the game was virtually over, but Stanford refused to give up. They took our kickoff in the third period and marched straight to a touchdown. The dynamiting Grayson, whom we were never able to stop, Bones Hamilton and Buck Van Dellen, powered to the score, with Van Dellen going over. That made it 22 to 13 as Moscrip failed to convert, but with our line holding well, Stanford never got closer.

Late in the third period, Francis intercepted another Stanford pass that led to our final touchdown. The six-pointer came when Howell passed to Hutson on the Stanford 30 and the eel-hipped, glue-fingered Don, who went on to prove himself the greatest end of our time, dashed the other 20 without difficulty. Smith placekicked the goal and the scoring in the 1935 Battle of the Roses ended.

On the field that day were possibly more great players than a college game had ever seen together. Alabama was represented by three All-Americas of 1934, Howell, Hutson and Bill Lee. Smith gained All-America the following year. Stanford had Grayson, Hamilton, Moscrip and Bob Reynolds. Smith and Hamilton were unsung heroes as blocking backs. Bryant for Alabama and Topping for Stanford were great.

Larry Rouble, of Stanford, was the outstanding lineman of the game.

But it was Dixie Howell who stole the show. Against a team famous for its driving power, he gained 111 yards rushing, topping even the bruising Grayson. He completed nine of the 12 passes he attempted. But it is for cooly standing out there with a ball poised for flight that he will always be remembered by those who saw the memorable game—my greatest game by my greatest team.

The lineup:

ALABAMA (29)	pos.	STANFORD (13)
Hutson	le	Moscrip
Whatley	lt	Reynolds
Marr	lg	Adams
Francis	c	Muller
Morrow	rg	Rouble
Lee	rt	Callaway
Bryant	re	Topping
Smith	qb	Alustiza
Howell	lh	Van Dellen
Angelich	rh	Hamilton
Demyanovich	fb	Grayson

Alabama .... 0—22—0—7——29
Stanford .... 7—0—6—0——13

Touchdowns: *Alabama*—Howell, 2, Hutson, 2. *Stanford*—Grayson, Van Dellen.

Field Goal: *Alabama*—Riley Smith (Placement)

Points after touchdowns: *Alabama*—Smith, 2. *Stanford*—Moscrip.

Substitutions: *Alabama*—H. Walker, Gandy, J. Walker, McGahey, Baswell, Danuletti, Peters, Dahlkamp, A. White, Dildy, Moye, Campbell, Goldberg, R. White, Stapp, Boozer. *Stanford* —Monsaive, Smith, Schott, Trompas, Lettunich, Callahan, Walton, Black, Brandin, Anderson, Maentz, Reisner, White, Anderson.

Referee—Bob Evans, Milliken; Umpire—Cort Majors, California. Linesman—G. M. Phillips, Georgia Tech. Field Judge—R. J. Ducote, Auburn.

GLENN SCOBIE (POP) WARNER

(*Cornell, '96*)

GEORGIA, 1895-1896.

CORNELL, 1897-1898.

CARLISLE INDIANS, 1899-1903.

CORNELL, 1904-1906.

CARLISLE, 1907-1914.

PITTSBURGH, 1915-1923.

STANFORD, 1924-1932.

TEMPLE, 1933-1938.

SAN JOSE STATE, 1939-1940.

Pop Warner ranks second in point of service to football with 46 years of coaching behind him. Only Amos Alonzo Stagg covered so long a span of brilliant, colorful gridiron drama. As a coach, too, Warner is regarded as one of the greatest, and it was only in 1947, seven years after his retirement from active coaching that he was honored by the Touchdown Club of New York for his excellent service to the game he loved.

Warner's victories were many and his football innovations lasting. He is credited with inventing and installing more formations and plays than any other coach. He invented the single and double-wingback formations, the crouching start, and the clipping block, among other defensive and offensive maneuvers, and these will live forever along with the name of Warner in football.

The career of Pop Warner began as a guard on Cornell's teams of 1892, 1893 and 1894. He captained the last of those elevens and won honorable mention on Walter Camp's original All-America that year. His thirteen years of coaching the Carlisle Indians produced some of the greatest stories ever written in football. He coached the mighty Jim Thorpe, regarded by many as the outstanding football player of all time, and his other Indian stars—Wauseka-Prince-Seneca-Hudson-Johnson-Exedine-Guyon-Welch—all helped inscribe an unusual chapter in the history of the gridiron. At Pittsburgh, he won 33 games without a defeat or a tie from 1915 through part of 1919.

Stanford's football glory dates with the arrival of Warner in 1924. It was there that he brought forth and developed the great Ernie Nevers, who is classed with Thorpe among the all-time fullbacks.

Warner was a showman as well as a football coach—a pioneer who kept up with the times.

POP WARNER
Stanford 20, California 20.
CALIFORNIA MEMORIAL STADIUM, NOVEMBER 22, 1924.

This was a game I didn't win but after 46 years of coaching I still call it my greatest day in football.

I've had other big days at Carlisle, with Jim Thorpe and the great Indian players like Al Wauseka, Albert Exedine, Bemis Pince, at Pittsburgh, with three undefeated teams in a row and players like Jock Sutherland and Bob Peck, but I can't forget that game against California in 1924. It was perhaps a new era in football for me, and for Stanford, too, where I now make my home.

I came to Stanford as head coach with a tough job ahead of me. Stanford was weak, woefully weak, and had been the doormat of the Pacific Coast Conference for some time. The year 1924 was my first year there and it was my misfortune to arrive at a time when California was ruling the roost with its "Wonder Team" as the writers called it. Under the able coaching of Andy Smith, the old Penn fullback, California had consistently beaten Stanford in their "Big Game." Naturally, we wanted to win against the Bears, and I don't think a team took the field with a stronger motive, or greater desire for victory than this Stanford team of 1924.

The "breaks" were against us. Our great halfback that year, Norm Cleveland, around whom our attack was centered, was declared ineligible. California insisted he be barred because Cleveland had played two minutes in a freshman game. His loss, coupled with

Pop Warner.

that of our mighty fullback, Ernie Nevers, who had suffered two broken ankles the week before, handicapped us severely. But we fought all the harder in a game that Walter Camp called the greatest he'd ever witnessed.

California was a heavy favorite and few, if any, gave us a chance to down the Bears or even come close. We had no plan of attack other than to do our best and we started with a vigor that even surprised me. Stanford kicked two goals from the field in the first half to lead California, 6 to 0. Murray Cuddeback kicked them both, one a short placement and the other a titanic boot from the 47-yard line and it looked as though the Indians would get their revenge that day.

The power of the Blue and Gold, however, was not to be denied. Early in the second half, California roared to three touchdowns in quick succession. They shook Tut Imlay loose for a long run that set up one score, produced another on a pass from Dixon to Imlay, and smashed savagely, with passes helping, to the third, making it California 20, Stanford 6—with about five minutes to go.

The situation looked hopeless for the Indians. Many Stanford backers in the crowd of 77,000 in the stands paid off their bets and left the Stadium feeling that Stanford had no chance. But football games don't end until the final whistle blows. In this last five minutes of play Stanford completed two long passes, kicked the goals and tied the score—20 to 20. Those passes were thrown by Edward Walker, a substitute halfback who had played end all season and was supposed to have only little passing ability.

They did it on pure courage and determination. Few teams would continue to fight against such odds with only five minutes of play and two touchdowns to make, but this Big Red team did it.

They started from midfield after California was forced to kick. Solomon brought the punt back 15 yards and then caught a pass to put the ball on the 20. Jim Lawson ran seven more on an end-around and, when two plays failed to gain, they called for a pass to Ted Shipkey, the best forward pass receiver I ever coached. Throw a pass anywhere in his vicinity and Shipkey was sure to catch it. He would have made a great ball carrier if he had been placed in the backfield.

Walker got off a high, wobbly pass. Two California men were on top of Shipkey as the ball approached but Ted jumped in the air with an amazing spring. He crashed into Cockey Brown, bumped into the other California man but caught the ball miraculously for a touchdown. Cuddeback kicked the goal and it was California 20, Stanford 13.

Just a few minutes left. California kicked off. We lost the ball but got it back in an exchange of punts. It was Stanford's ball, first down and 95 yards to go—not an altogether encouraging picture with the clock whirling faster towards the final whistle.

Solomon picked up seven through center and Cliff Hey reeled off 32 yards more on a fake reverse. On another full spinner, Hey made 10 more but only seconds remained now—and only one thing to do. Walker faded back and shot an eight-yard pass to Cuddeback with just two seconds left. There was no stopping Cuddeback, whose kicking had kept us in the game. He raced for the touchdown, and with everything hinging on Cuddeback's kick—he made good— the game was tied.

That was a ball game greater than any other in my book of coaching. We won three Conference crowns at Stanford later and

Pop Warner admires his great teams at Haskell and Stanford.

went on to win twice in three tries in the Rose Bowl. The might of Stanford seemed to begin right there. In 1928, in another of my "great days," we razzle-dazzled a champion Army team into defeat.

"The Stanford Indians," said Will Rogers at a show that night, "looked bigger in football uniforms than the Cadets in coonskin coats. General Pershing left the game at half time because he heard they were going to call on him to play left end."

I've been fortunate to have coached two of the greatest players in football history—Thorpe and Nevers. They've asked me often who was greater. Thorpe was greater than any in an open field but Nevers could do more things and was more consistent. You can't pick between them. My all-time All-America would have Brick Muller, of California, and Frank Hinkey of Yale, at the ends; Fats Henry of W & J and Wauseka at tackle; Pudge Heffelfinger, of Yale, and Pince, at guard; Peck at center, and a backfield of Walter Eckersall, of Chicago, at quarter; Thorpe and Willie Heston in the halfback slots, and Nevers at fullback.

But for my one great day, I'll stick to the game my Stanford Indians pulled out into a tie against California's "Wonder Team."

The lineup:

STANFORD (20)	pos.	CALIFORNIA (20)
T. Shipkey	le	L. Mell
H. Shipkey	lt	White
Swan	lg	Lau
Baker	c	Horrell
Neill	rg	Carey
Johnson	rt	Cook
Lawson	re	Huber
Mitchell	qb	Carlson
Cuddeback	lh	Dixon
Kelly	rh	Imlay
Hey	fb	Young

Stanford .... 0—6—0—14——20
California .... 0—0—7—13——20

Touchdowns: *Stanford*—T. Shipkey, Cuddeback. *California*—Griffith, 2, Imlay.

Points after touchdowns: *Stanford*—Cuddeback, 2. *California*—Carlson, 2.

Field Goals: *Stanford*—Cuddeback, 2.

ROBERT (BOB) WATERFIELD
(*U.C.L.A., '45*)
LOS ANGELES RAMS, 1946-

Most Valuable Player in the National League in 1945 and run-ner-up for the same award the following year—not a bad first two years for a beginner in the tough professional football ranks.

Waterfield only approached greatness as a college player, al-though on occasion, he was a brilliant performer. His play led the Uclans into the Rose Bowl on January 1, 1943, their only appearance in the historic classic at Pasadena. They bowed out in a valiant battle with Georgia and a couple of fellows named Frank Sinkwich and Charley Trippi, but the final score was only 9 to 0.

In 1944, came the first sign of the future Waterfield. He was tenth nationally in offense, fourth in forward passing, and took the punting title with an amazing demonstration in both number and distance of punts—60 kicks averaging 42.9 per effort—perilously close to the all-time college high of 43.0 held by Auburn's Dick McGowan, set in 1939.

Against March Field, he got off a punt of 91 yards, and in the East-West game on January 1, 1945, he gave what is considered the greatest football game punting performance of all time. Five kicks traveled an average distance of 59.4 yards, with one kick going 80, a second 74, and a third 60 yards. Just to break the monotony, his passes accounted for both touchdowns in the West's 13–6 victory.

His play with the Los Angeles Rams, formerly Cleveland, has been sensational. He found a pass-receiver made to order for him in Jim Benton, and between them they led the Rams to their first and thus far only league championship, in 1945. In 1946, Waterfield topped the league in forward passing—over Sid Luckman, Sammy Baugh, Paul Governali, and other seasoned veterans.

BOB WATERFIELD
Los Angeles Rams 31, New York Giants 21.
NEW YORK, DECEMBER 1, 1946.

There's little hesitancy on my part when considering my greatest day in football—the game that gave me the greatest thrill. I have to choose the December 2, 1946, game in the Polo Grounds against the Giants. Yes, that one even over the Rams 15-14 victory over the Washington Redskins for Cleveland's first National League championship.

In 1945, my first year with the Rams, we won nine games and lost but one. We were favored to win the championship and that we did in a sub-zero setting in Cleveland. The fact that I passed to both our touchdowns and kicked an extra point that dramatically hit the top of the goal bar and bounced over—the right way—was indeed a thrill. But somehow the greatest feelings a guy seems to get come when you're the underdog and not expected to win. That Sammy Baugh, Washington's mighty passer "who can thread a needle with a pass," was hurt and didn't play most of the game in Cleveland Rams possibly was another factor in my picking the 1946 battle against odds and the Giants.

The Giants of 1946 needed one victory to clinch the Eastern Division title when they came up against us. When that day was done, they still needed that victory, which they got by trouncing the Redskins, 31 to 0, the following week.

Bob Waterfield is Number 1 Ram of Los Angeles despite his Number 7.

It was one of those days for me. Like a pitcher, I had control. I threw 29 passes that afternoon, gaining 312 yards as 22 of them were caught. A pitcher is no good without a catcher and I had three sure-fingered catchers—Jim Benton, Fred Gehrke and Bob Shaw around to make me look good.

Three of those passes went for touchdowns, two to Benton and one to Gehrke, and to make the day complete I added a field goal and four extra points.

Actually, the game was a lot closer than the score indicates. We didn't have a chance to breathe freely until the last minutes before the final gun. What really won the game for us, was getting the jump at the start. Before the Giants could concentrate their offensive or defensive, they were trailing 14 to 0. Early in the first quarter, we marched 76 yards for a touchdown, set up when Benton made a nice catch of my pass for a 31-yard gain and first down on the Giant five. From the three, two plays later, the Giants were fooled completely as I started what looked like a dash to my right. With their defense sucked over, I whirled and flung a pass to Gehrke, who fell across the goal line.

A fumble gave us the ball on the Giants' 43 shortly afterward. This time it was Benton, who caught 12 passes that day to fall two short of the league record, who took a 16-yarder to score.

Our visions of a runaway were quickly wiped out. Bill Paschal, one of the toughest runners in the league, took the kickoff and raced 54 yards with it. Then Frank Reagan pounded to our 16 from where Frank Filchock heaved a touchdown pass to Frank Liebel in the end zone.

We got that one back just before the end of the half, however. Again it was the astounding Benton ringing the payoff register, as he smothered a 10-yard pass that meant 21 to 7 in our favor at half time.

Those Giants battled furiously through a raging third period—scoreless until 35 seconds before it ended when Reagan slipped through on a great 52-yard dash to make the score 21 to 14.

The tide seemed to have turned but this must have been my day for luck was with us even as the Giants knocked on the door for the tying touchdown. Marching for what seemed certain to lead to a score, the Giants saw the usually glue-fingered Liebel take

Filchock's pass on our five—then drop it, when hit hard. Tommy Harmon recovered for us and we immediately drove to the Giants' five, where I dropped back and booted a field goal to cement the lead.

The Giants were a beaten team right then but they wouldn't admit it. With Filchock tossing 41 and then 19 yards to Reagan, they put the ball on our 26. Filchock passed again, this time to Howie Livingston, and it was 24 to 21.

Time was running out, and the game was clinched when Shaw picked up Ken Strong's onside kick designed to give the Giants the ball and raced 51 yards for the final touchdown.

It was a great victory for a team that had won only four, lost four, and tied one. That's why I pick it as my greatest day in football.

The lineup:
LOS ANGELES

(31)	pos.	New York (21)
Benton	le	Poole
Schultz	lt	Coulter
Matheson	lg	Dobelstein
Naumetz	c	Gladchuk
Lazetich	rg	Younce
Bouley	rt	White
Pritko	re	Howell
Waterfield	qb	Filipowicz
Gehrke	lh	Brown
Banta	rh	Livingston
West	fb	Strong
Los Angeles	14—7—0—10——31	
New York	7—0—7—7——21	

Touchdowns: *Los Angeles*—Benton, 2, Gehrke, Shaw (sub for Pritko). *New York*—Liebel (sub for Poole), Reagan (sub for Brown) Livingston.

Points after touchdowns: *Los Angeles*—Waterfield, 4. *New York*—Strong, 3.

Field Goal: *Los Angeles*—Waterfield.

Substitutions: *Rams*—Harmon, Ruthstrom, Hardy, Farmer, Holovak, Wilson, Strode, Hamilton, Shaw, Hickey, Johnson, Fawcett, Mergenthal, Lear, Eason, De Laur, Lavy, Harding.

Giants—Filchock, Soar, Hare, Franck, Paschal, Reagan, Hapes, Weiss, Mead, McCafferty, Liebel, Cope, Ragazzo, Carroll, Lunday, Tuttle, Edwards, DeFilippo, Palazzi.

Referee—R. Gibbs, St. Thomas. Umpire—Carl Brubaker, Ohio Wesleyan. Field Judge—Charles Sweeney, Notre Dame. Linesman—Daniel Tehan, Xavier.

E. E. (TAD) WIEMAN
(Michigan, '21)
MICHIGAN, 1921-1929.
MINNESOTA, 1930-1931.
PRINCETON, 1932-1942.
MAINE, 1946-   .

A reformed fullback, Tad Wieman is regarded as one of football's greatest line builders.

He was a fullback at Michigan in 1916 and 1917, in addition to being a Phi Beta Kappa student. He entered the Air Corps in 1917, and when he returned to the Wolverines in 1920, found himself a tackle. It was in the line that he eventually gained national recognition. All his teams have been powerful defensively.

Tad Wieman learned his football under such master strategists as "Hurry Up" Yost and Fritz Crisler and he added to his lore a mind as keen as the proverbial razor. While he has rarely had a wealth of material to work with, his teams have always been dangerous.

Wieman's war record did not end with World War I. He returned to active duty in 1943 as chief of the Army's College Physical Training program. Always on the lookout for football, he received leave to help Lou Little at Columbia in 1944 and 1945.

Always popular with players and fellow coaches, Wieman returned to coaching in 1946 at little Maine University in Orono. The size of the University or the numbers of its student body is unimportant in collegiate football, however. Wieman was elected president of the Football Coaches of America in 1946.

TAD WIEMAN
Michigan 21, Ohio State 0.
ANN ARBOR, MICH., OCTOBER 22, 1927.

Michigan 21, Ohio State 0. There's a score I'll never forget. I couldn't if I wanted to because there were too many important connecting circumstances. Which was the most important, I haven't figured out to this day. All I can do is relate the details.

That October 22nd back in 1927 wasn't just a usual October 22nd. For the little town of Ann Arbor—the college town where the University of Michigan makes its home—it was to be a great day. And it was up to me, as coach of the football team, to see that it wasn't spoiled.

That was Dedication Day for Michigan's new stadium, a mammoth structure that seated 86,000. As it neared completion, there were many skeptics who didn't believe it could be filled. But when applications for the Ohio State dedication game were filed on September 1, the Stadium was over-subscribed on the first day.

In those days, 86,000 people formed a tremendous and almost unheard of football crowd. Yet, here it was six weeks before game time and two weeks before the teams even started pre-season practice and the contest was a sellout.

My task, in view of the expected turnout, was a tremendous one. More so, when considering that Ohio State, in those days, was our principal rival. If that wasn't enough to keep me awake nights,

I reminded myself that I had just succeeded the great Fielding Yost as Michigan coach and this was to be my first big game.

Oh how I kept wishing I had Benny Friedman around to toss passes to Benny Oosterbaan. Those two had formed one of the greatest aerial combinations of all time, but Friedman had been graduated. I guess I was lucky, at that, to have Oosterbaan captaining the team. After all, how much could a three-time All-America end hurt you?

With Friedman gone, I naturally looked around for someone who could get that ball to Oosterbaan. At least near him, because Benny could catch anything within reach and sometimes out of it. Anyway, I found a clever little halfback by the name of Louis Gilbert. Gilbert was no Friedman, but he and Oosterbaan still formed a terrific threat.

But this story is not one of Gilbert passing to Oosterbaan. It's a tale of Oosterbaan passing to Gilbert. During my search for a Friedman successor, I'd experimented with Oosterbaan throwing the ball. He was such a fine athlete, why not let him pass? Well, the great end showed me just enough to give me the shot of optimism I needed for the crucial Ohio State game.

We planned and planned for the Buckeyes. And it all boiled down to the strategic use of Oosterbaan as a passer. This was to be an even game. That's the way it looked on paper. But if our plans worked . . . ?

Well, to make a long story short, they did. There was nothing spectacular about the game itself, except that Oosterbaan flipped two touchdown passes and a lateral to Gilbert, who scored all 21 points.

The first came in the second period. Oosterbaan ducked back from his end position, took the ball from the tailback and flung 25 yards to Gilbert, who ran 15 more. In the third quarter, Benny repeated the maneuver with a 48-yard play on which Gilbert partially fell making the catch and stumbled across the goal line. Then came the fourth quarter lateral, with Gilbert straight-arming two tacklers on his way to a touchdown.

Three plays worked just as we planned them. And, with Gilbert's tremendous punts keeping Ohio State bottled in its territory throughout, we made Dedication Day a victorious one.

Fielding Yost had entrusted me, his assistant, with carrying on Michigan's football fortunes. Oosterbaan and Gilbert gave me a good start and one I'll never forget.

The Lineup:

OHIO STATE

(0)	pos.	MICHIGAN (21)
Alber	le	Oosterbaan
Raskowski	lt	Pommerening
Meyer	lg	Palmeroli
Ullery	c	Bovard
Cox	rg	Baer
Messer	rt	Gabel
Rowan	re	Nyland
Marek	qb	Hoffmann
Grim	lh	Miller
Huston	rh	Gilbert
Ohsner	fb	Rich

Ohio State .... 0—0—0—0—0
Michigan .... 0—7—7—7——21

Touchdowns: *Michigan*—Gilbert, 3.

Points after touchdowns: *Michigan*—Gilbert, 3.

Substitutions: *Michigan*—Sullo, Parker, Domhoff, Harrigan, Husten, Gembis, Fuller, Puckelwartz, Whittle. *Ohio State*—Eby, Ackerman, Smith, Young, Cudil, Kriss, Fouch, Bell, McClure.

Referee—Masker, Northwestern. Umpire—Haines, Yale. Field Judge—Young, Illinois Wesleyan. Linesman—Huston, Parsons.

ROBERT C. (BOB) ZUPPKE

(*Wisconsin, '05*)

MUSKEGON, MICH., HIGH SCHOOL, 1906-1910.
OAK PARK, ILL., HIGH SCHOOL, 1910-1913.
ILLINOIS, 1913-1941.

Philosopher, artist and coach, Bob Zuppke of Illinois ranks among the top coaches in football history. His creed as a coach was simple:

"There are times you can lose 'em all and still look good in every game you lost. There are times you can win and not look good at all.

"There is only one thing in football that is more important than winning. That is to leave the field with your opponent's respect, win or lose."

Zuppke stood for courage, clean play, hard play, decency.

At Wisconsin, Zuppke's contribution to the Badger football fortunes was two years of play—as a scrub. He went on to Muskegon High as teacher of history, and coach of football, track, baseball and cross-country. As coach at Oak Park, his teams lost one game in three years and were National High School champions in 1912. His record at Illinois included six Western Conference championships, a National championship in 1927, and a back by the name of Harold (Red) Grange, considered by many the greatest ball carrier of all time. The Galloping Ghost's feat of five touchdowns in five plays against Michigan in 1924 stands out as one of the most amazing running exhibitions on any football field.

A master of football trickery and deception, Zuppke invented such plays as the "flea flicker," "whoa back," "razzle-dazzle" and "flying trapeze." He retired from active coaching at the end of the 1941 season, although he returned to tutor the Chicago All-Stars and the Philadelphia All-Americans in 1942. He spends most of his time at Champaign, Illinois, pursuing his art work.

Zuppke of Illinois is a football immortal.

BOB ZUPPKE
Illinois 14, Minnesota 9.
MINNEAPOLIS, NOVEMBER 4, 1916.

Minnesota had what was known as the perfect team. Illinois had a very mediocre team. Illinois left Champaign on a Wednesday night to meet the Gophers on Saturday, not a very pleasant prospect after a glance at the Minnesota record:

> Minnesota 67, Iowa 0.
> Minnesota 81, South Dakota 0.
> Minnesota 54, Wisconsin 0.
> Minnesota 49, Chicago 0.

The Golden Gophers had left a tremendous impression. Dr. Henry (Harry) Williams was their coach, and this team was reminiscent of Yost's famous point-a-minute teams of the past.

The boys had buck fever even when Minnesota was mentioned. Bart Macomber, All-America halfback of our championship team of 1915, was captain. We had lost such men as Ralph (Slowey) Chapman, Harold Pogue, Potsy Clark, through graduation, and our 1916 eleven had started off with losses to Colgate, Ohio State and Chicago, and a scoreless tie with Wisconsin.

Ring Lardner predicted a 49-0 defeat for Illinois.

Walter Camp had been specially invited along with other football experts to see Minnesota's greatest team. He saw the game from a small, special grandstand.

Bob Zuppke reviews his portrait and admires his prize subject—
the fabulous Red Grange.

Howard Jones was the coach of Iowa that year, and Dr. P. W. Whitington, of Harvard, coach at Wisconsin. This was their first impression of Big Ten football.

This was the setting that Saturday as 25,000 people jammed the old wooden stands at Minneapolis to see the Gophers roll on in a game which they were calling a cinch at 20 to 1, and quoting 10 to 1 we wouldn't score. Friday, the day before the game, I scrimmaged the boys and it was small wonder that I told them to forget the game and to go out and have a good time that night. Friday night they went to a show and stayed up till about 11:30, which is late for anyone in training.

Illinois had nothing to lose and any score under 50 by the Gophers would apparently have been a morale victory as everyone in Minneapolis told us the best we could hope for was to hold the score down to 50 to 0. George Halas, now owner of the Chicago Bears, was an end on the Illinois team that year—he was on crutches for this game.

The result of that game is still considered football's greatest upset and the Chicago *Tribune* had this screaming headline over its account of the game:

"HOLD TIGHT WHEN YOU READ THIS."

The game was a story of a fighting Illinois team that took advantage of the breaks and used every trick in the book to maintain an early lead. We were later accused of using delaying tactics and while it is true that shoe strings and shoulder guards probably did break during the game, that happened because of the fury of the battle and not because "Fabius the Delayer" helped to direct the game from the bench.

Macomber was a great halfback that day. He kicked off with the ball lying flat on the ground. Minnesota fumbled on the five-yard line but recovered. They were forced to punt—Wyman kicked to Dutch Sternaman, our right halfback. He caught the punt and ran 10 yards to the Gopher 45-yard mark. A fullback smash gained nothing, and then Illinois called for a spread formation, a new play in which the linemen spread out six yards from each other—the backfield doing the same in square formation. This was the turning point of the game.

Minnesota didn't know whether to play opposite the man or opposite the hole between our linemen. Macomber then passed to

Sternaman for a 25-yard gain, and on the next play ran over center for the first touchdown, on a quarterback sneak from the T-formation. Macomber also kicked the extra point and it was 7 to 0. The mighty Gophers had yielded their first score of the season.

Minnesota elected to receive and, on third down, Wyman tried a pass to Baston. The combination of Wyman to Baston is considered to this day one of the greatest pass combinations in football history. The pass went wild and left end Kraft of Illinois was there to intercept. He ran 55 yards for the second touchdown and Macomber's kick made it 14 to 0.

The Gophers fought back desperately and in the third period, they made it 14 to 9. We were playing this game with the original eleven men. The Gophers were strong, with plenty of reserves, and we had to do everything to keep them from getting the ball in the fourth period. Somehow, we managed it, and the mighty myth of Minnesota was exploded by a team that on the record had no right in the same Stadium.

After the game, the crowd was so stunned that they forgot to go home until a cloud burst drove them out of the stands, including Walter Camp and his experts in the special little stand, which was completely blown away. "After us, the deluge."

I must call this, without hesitation, my greatest day in football—even over the thrill of seeing our Galloping Ghost, Red Grange, run wild for Illinois in 1923, 1924 and 1925. I've been fortunate to coach great teams in my career and great players like Grange, Macomber, Novak and Carney. Carney was as great an end as ever lived, and, on my All-America team, he would be on one end and Don Hutson on the other. Novak would be at tackle with Duke Slater of Iowa, and Yale's Pudge Heffelfinger would share guard honors with Jack Cannon of Notre Dame. Bulldog Turner would be at center and the "dream" backfield would have Indian Jim Thorpe at quarterback, Willie Heston and Grange would hold down the halfback positions and the great Bronko Nagurski would reign at fullback.

The lineup:
ILLINOIS
(14)   pos.   MINNESOTA (9)
Kraft . . . . le . . . . Baston
Rundquist . . . . . . lt . . . . Townley

O. Petty ....lg....... Sinclair
Schlauderman ....c....... J. Hansen
Stewart ....rg....... Mayer
R. Petty ....rt....... Hauser
Christenson .....re....... Buckley
Macomber .....qb....... Long
Sternaman .....lh....... Sprafka
Anderson ....rh....... H. Hansen
Knopp ....fb....... Wyman
Illinois ....14—0—0—0——14
Minnesota ....0—0—9—0——9

Touchdowns: *Illinois*—Macomber, Kraft. *Minnesota*—Sprafka.

Safety: *Minnesota*—Sternaman.

Points after touchdowns: *Illinois*—Macomber, 2. *Minnesota*—Baston.

Substitutes: *Illinois*—none. *Minnesota*—Carlson, Anderson.

Referee—Means, Pennsylvania. Umpire—Juneau, Wisconsin.

Field Judge—Grady, Northwestern. Linesman—Graham, Grinnell.